CW00494668

The Lordly Ones

By the same author

THE HOLLOW CROWNS
A History of the Battles of the Wars of the Roses

THE DECEIVERS
The solution to the murder of the Princes in the Tower

The Lordly Ones

*"How beautiful they are, the lordly ones, who dwell in the hills . . .
They laugh and are glad and are terrible; When their lances
shake every green reed quivers. How beautiful they are, how
beautiful, the lordly ones in the hollow hills . . ."*

**[The Enchanted Forest.
Fiona Macleod.]**

*A History of the Neville Family and their part in the
Wars of the Roses*

GEOFFREY RICHARDSON

This edition published 1998

by Baildon Books
P.O. Box 107, SHIPLEY, W. Yorks BD17 6UR

Copyright © 1998 Geoffrey Richardson

All rights reserved. No part of this publication may be
reproduced, stored in a retrieval system, or transmitted
in any form or by any means, electronic, mechanical,
photocopying, recording, or otherwise, without the prior
permission of the publishers.

Printed in Great Britain by
Pennine Printing Services Ltd.
Ripponden, West Yorkshire, England

ISBN 0 9527621 2 9

*Since – yet again – this is "my last book", I
dedicate it to my children, Jane and John,
to my granddaughter, Gemma, and ever and
again to the fountain from whence they - and
all my other true joys in life - have sprung,
my lovely wife, Betty.*

CONTENTS

Illustrations and Maps

Portraits of Edward IV, Richard III are reproduced by kind permission of the Society of Antiquaries of London. All other illustrations, Coats of Arms and signatures are provided by Geoffrey Wheeler of London. Original Battlemaps from "The Hollow Crowns" were drawn by Roy Barton, NDD, ATD. New Battlemaps and cover were drawn by Terry Brown.

The Nevilles in the 15th Century

RALPH NEVILLE, 6th Baron Neville, 1st E. of Westmorland, d. 1425

=

(1) Margaret, dau. of Hugh, 2nd E. of Stafford

(2) Joan Beaufort, dau. of John of Gaunt.

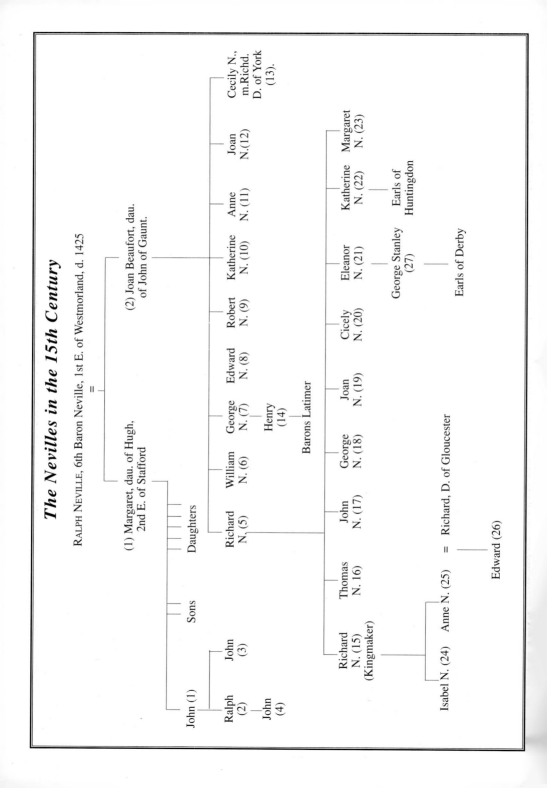

John (1)

Ralph (2)

John (4)

John (3)

Sons

Daughters

Richard N. (5)

William N. (6)

George N. (7) — Henry (14) — Barons Latimer

Edward N. (8)

Robert N. (9)

Katherine N. (10)

Anne N. (11)

Joan N.(12)

Cecily N., m.Richd. D. of York (13).

Richard N. (15) (Kingmaker)

Thomas N. 16

John N. (17)

George N. (18)

Joan N. (19)

Cicely N. (20)

Eleanor N. (21) — George Stanley (27) — Earls of Derby

Katherine N. (22) — Earls of Huntingdon

Margaret N. (23)

Isabel N. (24)

Anne N. (25) = Richard, D. of Gloucester

Edward (26)

NOTES

1. LANCASTRIAN (ELDER BRANCH OF NEVILLES)

1. John, d. 1423; m. Elizabeth, dau. of Thomas Holland, Earl of Kent.
2. Ralph Neville, 2nd Earl of Westmorland, d. 1484; m. Elizabeth Percy, dau. of Hotspur.
3. John Neville, created Lord Neville 1459, killed at Towton 1461; m. Anne Holland, his nephew's widow; took prominent part in family feud.
4. John Neville, killed at St. Albans 1455; m. Anne Holland, dau. of John, Duke of Exeter.

2. YORKIST (YOUNGER BRANCH OF NEVILLES)

5. Richard Neville, Earl of Salisbury, beheaded 1460, after Wakefield; m. Alice, dau. and heir of Thomas Montacute, Earl of Salisbury.
6. William Neville, Lord Fauconberg, created Earl of Kent 1461, d. 1463; m. Joan, dau. of Thomas, Lord Fauconberg.
7. George Neville, Baron Latimer, d. 1469; m. Elizabeth, dau. of Richard Beauchamp, 5th Earl of Warwick.
8. Edward Neville, d. 1476; m. Elizabeth, dau. and heir of Richard Beauchamp, Baron of Abergavenny.
9. Robert Neville, d. 1457; Bishop of Salisbury 1427, Bishop of Durham 1438.
10. Katherine Neville, m. (1) John Mowbray, 2nd Duke of Norfolk, and (4) John Woodville, brother of Elizabeth Woodville.
11. Anne Neville, m. (1) Humphrey Stafford, 1st Duke of Buckingham, killed at Northampton 1460.
12. Joan Neville, a nun.
13. Cicely Neville, m. Richard Plantagenet, Duke of York.
14. Henry Neville, killed at Edgecote 1469.
15. Richard Neville, 1450 Earl of Warwick (the king-maker), and in 1460 Earl of Salisbury, killed at Barnet 1471; m. Anne, dau. and heir of Richard Beauchamp, 5th Earl of Warwick.
16. Thomas Neville, killed at Wakefield 1460.
17. John Neville, Lord Montagu 1461, Earl of Northumberland 1464, Marquis Montagu 1470, killed at Barnet 1471.
18. George Neville, d. 1476; Bishop of Exeter 1458, Archbishop of York 1465.
19. Joan Neville, m. William Fitz-Alan, Earl of Arundel.
20. Cecily Neville, m. (1) Henry Beauchamp, Duke of Warwick, d. 1446; (2) John Tiptoft, Earl of Worcester, beheaded 1470.
21. Eleanor Neville, m. Thomas, Lord Stanley, created Earl of Derby 1485.
22. Katherine Neville, betrothed to William Bonvile, Lord Harington, killed at Wakefield 1460; m. William, Lord Hastings, beheaded 1483.
23. Margaret Neville, m. John de Vere, 13th Earl of Oxford.
24. Isabel Neville, d. 1476, m. George, Duke of Clarence.
25. Anne Neville, d. 1485, m. (1) Edward, Prince of Wales, slain at Tewkesbury 1471; m. (2) Richard Plantagenet, Duke of Gloucester (Richard III).

26. Edward Plantagenet, d. 1484.
27. George Stanley, Lord Strange, d. 1497.

**Effigy of Ralph Neville and his two wives
Joan Beaufort [l] and Margaret Stafford [r]**

[Drawn by Charles A. Stothard]

(Geoffrey Wheeler)

CHAPTER ONE

Beginnings . . .

The Wars of the Roses, as they came to be called, were an internecine conflict between two branches of the House of Plantagenet : York and Lancaster, fought over a period of 30 years, to restore and maintain the rightful succession of the senior branch - York - to the throne of England.

They also provided a bloody platform for the settling of deadly rivalries between two other great houses which, like the Plantagenets, were closely related by blood, and whose irreconcilable enmity and unquenchable thirst for power provided as much driving force for the Wars as did the struggle for the crown between the main participants. These families were the Beauforts - the bastard line springing from a doubly adulterous liaison between John of Gaunt, third surviving son of Edward III, and Katherine Swynford - and the Nevilles, whose loyalties were divided between York and Lancaster with, strangely, the branch which allied itself most strongly with the claims of York descending from Joan Beaufort, daughter of John of Gaunt.

Starting their expansion in the early 13th Century, the Nevilles gradually came to hold much land in the south of England, the English Midlands, and into Wales, but their main wealth and strength stemmed always from the northern lands which they dominated from great castles, notably Middleham, Barnard, Raby and Sheriff Hutton. The original fountain-head of the family was Robert Fitzmaldred, Lord of Raby who, in the reign of King John (1199-1216) married Isabella Neville, daughter of Robert's neighbour Geoffrey Neville of Brancepeth. Through the eldest son of this union, another Geoffrey, the Teesdale lands of the Fitzmaldreds were united with the larger Neville inheritance around Durham and Geoffrey took his mother's name, the Fitzmaldred title falling into disuse.

The new line of Lords of Raby made no great, initial impact on the history of their time. They served their monarch as required, against the Scots - principally - and the French; they quarrelled with their peers from time to time and occasionally bickered with their feudal lord, the Bishop of Durham. In short, they were typical   Barons of England, proud and disorderly, acquisitive of lands and titles, well-versed in military matters but content to draw increases in strength and wealth from marriage alliances rather than success in battle. Nevertheless, on one signal occasion, a Neville led the English vanwards against the Scots and subsequently commemorated the victory by raising the memorial monument from which the battle would take its name : Neville's Cross.

On August 26, 1346, Edward III had inflicted a crushing defeat on the French at Crecy, and Philip VI had called on his ally, David II, the young King of Scotland, to attack across the border and draw English attention (and reinforcements) away from the fields of France. David, at 23 years of age, was eager to find his first-blooding in battle and his men were likewise ever-responsive to thoughts of the rich plunder awaiting their attention a few miles south of the border. Thus, King David was able to recruit a large host very quickly and the raiding army crossed the Cumberland border in early October and by the 16th of that month had carved a bloody path eastwards across northern England to the gates of Durham. Here the reivers encamped and disported themselves, not realising that a substantial English force had been gathered by the Archbishop of York and, led by the current Lord of Raby, Ralph Neville, and Harry Percy, Lord of Northumberland, was already fast-closing on the merry-making Scots.

On the 17th of October, the Scottish King was warned of the English army's approach by a routed raiding party commanded by Sir William Douglas, who had run into the English advance guard three miles northeast of Bishop Auckland and fled, making a running fight of it to Sunderland Bridge, where they had finally evaded their pursuers. David scorned advice from his more experienced leaders that retreat with the loot already gathered would be the sensible policy and, instead, arrayed his men for battle in three divisions across Crossgate Moor. Their English adversaries drew up in a single division, facing the Scots at some 500 yards distance, with their flanks protected by a river-ravine on the left and a sharp slope on the right.

Made bold by their successes to date, the Scots' right flank division (their vanguard) opened the attack, but ran into difficult ground to their front and had to move leftwards, thus compressing the space available to the centre division led by King David. Nevertheless, the combined divisions made some head against the English front line initially, but then emerged onto open ground, ideal for cavalry, in which arm Neville's force was particularly strong. Lord Ralph led his horse in a vigorous charge which crushed his

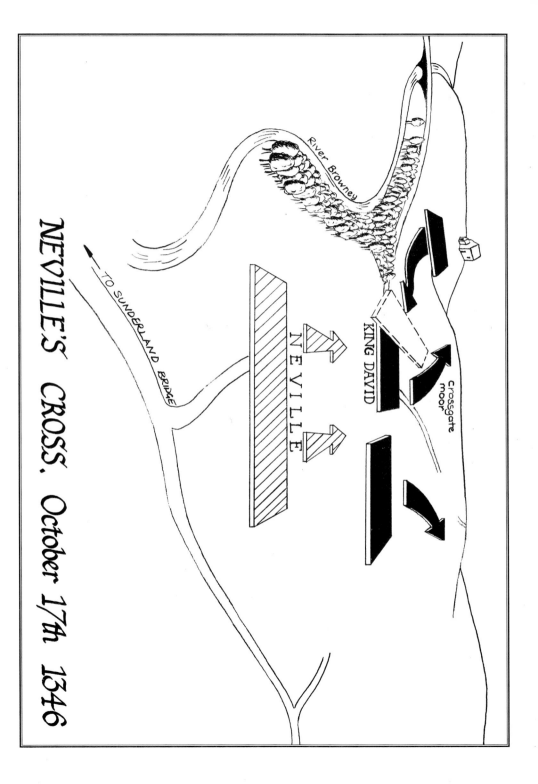

NEVILLE'S CROSS, October 17th 1346

River Browney

TO SUNDERLAND BRIDGE

NEVILLE

KING DAVID

crossgate moor

opponents' advance and left the Scottish King fighting a hopeless rearguard action, while his army melted away around him. David was wounded and himself fled the field, but was captured, according to tradition, under the bridge crossing the Browney just west of Arbour House, and spent several years imprisoned in the Tower.

Thus, the Nevilles added military victor's laurels to their existing distinctions, but they had - always, it seemed - been more clearly distinguishable from their coequals for two other particular attributes: they were extraordinarily fertile, regularly producing families of ten or more children, the majority of whom survived to adulthood, and they were unusually clever in marrying themselves and their heirs to single surviving scions of wealthy, landed families. It was the combination of these two factors which had led to the power, wealth and connections of the Nevilles spreading steadily throughout England, even though the main concentration of their wealth continued to be in the northern counties.

In the reign of Henry III, son of King John, another Robert Neville had married into the Mitford family and thereby acquired a Northumbrian Barony in the valley of the Wansbeck. Robert's son, of the same name, married Mary of Middleham and, in her right, became Lord of the castle which would be the main base of his family's future power in the north and which came with title to manors running for miles along the Ure and south-westwards down along Coverdale. His son Ralph added to his patrimony by marrying the heiress of Clavering (in Essex) who brought much more valuable lands along the Northumberland coast around Warkworth into the family holdings, and Ralph's son, John, after a first marriage to a younger daughter of the Percies of Northumberland, secured for his second bride, Elizabeth, wealthy heiress of the Latimers with large holdings in Bedford and Buckinghamshire.

By this time, the Nevilles had become the greatest Lords in the North, richer and stronger even than the Percies of Alnwick. They held nearly eighty manors in half a dozen counties, but their main holdings were in North Yorkshire and Durham, centred on their two main fortresses, Middleham and Raby. At the King's call, they could put 14 knights with 300 men-at-arms and 300 archers into the field for service in foreign parts and, against the Scots, the Lord of Middleham would raise 2,000 well-armed and armoured men without difficulty.

As the 14th Century drew to a close, the Nevilles were recognised as a great power in the land, and therefore worthy even of Royal patronage to ensure future support and enduring loyalty. Richard II, son of the Black Prince, and eager to increase and ensure his support against the possibility of insurrection in favour of the Lancastrian branch of Edward III's extensive and quarrelsome brood, felt it politic to raise Ralph Neville to the dignity of an Earldom in 1397. The bulk of Earl Ralph's holdings in Yorkshire and Durham, however, were not conveniently located to provide him with his new title. York was reserved to the royal family and the 'Jarldom' of Durham went to the Bishop of that See as the traditional defender of his county against the Scots since the days of the Conqueror and before. The Percies had Northumberland and so Ralph, faute de mieux, became the first Earl of Westmorland, where, in fact, he held not a single acre of ground. Together with his new title, however, Earl Ralph received the royal honour of Penrith, thus giving a somewhat firmer basis for his new-found distinction.

Unhappily for King Richard, the new title weighed little against the fact that Ralph's second wife was Joan Beaufort, only daughter in the illegitimate brood produced by John of Gaunt and Katherine Swynford, and when Ralph's half-brother-in-law, Henry Bolingbroke, landed at Ravenspur in 1399 to claim the throne, Ralph Neville was among the first to join with him. Following Richard's forced abdication, Bolingbroke - once Earl of Derby, now Henry IV of England - made Ralph Neville Earl Marshal in place of the Mowbray Dukes of Norfolk, whose hereditary role this had been.

The new Earl Marshal had a successful career in support of his preferred King. When Henry IV, who was ever short of money, tried to improve his finances by taking over the ransoming of Scots prisoners captured at Homildon Hill (September 14, 1402) by the Percies' greatest champion, Harry Hotspur, the growing discord between the Northumberland family and the crown erupted into open conflict. Hotspur, with his father, the Earl, and his uncle, Sir Thomas Percy, created Earl of Worcester by Richard II, gathered men in the northeast and in Cheshire, and drew still further strength from Welshmen joining as the rebel army moved towards Lichfield.

When the Northumberland men reached Shrewsbury, they met an even larger host led by the King and his eldest son, Harry of Monmouth (later Henry V) in which was arrayed, in full warlike panoply, Ralph Neville, Earl of Westmorland, with nearly 2,000 men at his back. Outnumbered and outfought, the rebel army of Northumberland after some initial success, was pressed back in confusion as Prince Henry's division outflanked them and when Harry Hotspur was killed by an arrow, the Percies' host dissolved, broke and ran. The rebellion was over, the House of Lancaster was firmly established on England's throne, and Ralph Neville, and his House, were equally firmly entrenched in the favour of the King he had twice aided at critical junctures.

It is ironic to reflect that sons and grandsons of Earl Ralph would, fifty years and more after Shrewsbury, play a key role in the disenthronement of the grandson of Henry Bolingbroke and in the deaths of other of his closest relatives who had become the main support of the House of Lancaster. But this was the way of the world in the troubled times which have come down to us as the Wars of the Roses.

Middleham Castle in the 18th Century
(Geoffrey Wheeler)

CHAPTER TWO

"And if a house be divided against itself,
that house cannot stand ..."

(Mark 3.25)

By his first wife Margaret, daughter of Hugh, Earl of Stafford, Ralph Neville had nine children. His second marriage was even more fruitful with no less than 14 offspring resulting from Ralph's union with the royal Princess, Joan Beaufort, and the greater favour which Earl Ralph showed to his second line of heirs was to cause a sharp rift in the family which was subsequently reflected in the taking of opposite sides in the coming civil wars in England, with, strangely, the children and grandchildren of Lancastrian Joan Beaufort providing much of the early strength of the Yorkist cause.

Following the family tradition, Ralph arranged advantageous marriages for all his children and grandchildren. His first family by Margaret of Stafford, he was able to marry to heirs and heiresses of local families of name and rank : Ferrers, Mauley, Dacre, Scrope and Kyme. But for his younger branch, who had the blood royal in their veins, he was able to arrange more ambitious and advantageous unions. His oldest son in the second family, Richard, married the heiress of the Salisbury Earldom, Alice Montacute, and took the title on his father-in-law's death in the war with France. The second son, William, became Lord Fauconberg (sometimes, Fauconbridge) and, after signal service to Edward IV at Ferrybridge and Towton in 1461, would be created Earl of Kent. The other sons became by various ways and means, Lord Latimer, Lord Abergavenny, and Bishop of Salisbury, subsequently translated to the much more powerful See of Durham.

The daughters of Earl Ralph's second marriage were hardly less fortunate than their brothers. Katherine became Duchess of Norfolk, and Anne, Duchess of Buckingham, while the baby of the family, Cecily, called the Rose of Raby for her great beauty, became the child-bride of Richard Plantagenet, Duke of York, shortly before Ralph's death, and by him would bear two future Kings of England, Edward IV and Richard III.

Initially, the two Neville broods lived peaceably enough together under the strict tutelage of Earl Ralph, a tall, imposing figure, who affected an unfashionable moustache and developed a limp late in life. However, on his death in 1425 in his 62nd year, it was found that he had left the ancient Neville lands around Durham and Raby to his grandson Ralph, heir to the Earldom through the prior death of old Ralph's eldest son, John, but that the bulk of his property including the vast holdings in north Yorkshire were entrusted to his widow, Joan Beaufort, and, through her, to the junior branch of the family.

Richard Neville, eldest son of Joan Beaufort, became Earl of Salisbury in his wife's right in 1428 and took possession of the Montacute heritage which was largely in Wiltshire and Hampshire. He was summoned to the following parliament in his new dignity as Earl of Salisbury in 1429, where, coincidentally, the new Earl Ralph of Westmorland also made his debut appearance.

In the first years of the following decade, bad blood between the two sections of the family progressively showed itself. The Westmorland branch became increasingly resentful of the comparatively greater wealth of Joan Beaufort and her family, which they regarded as a part of their own patrimony, thrown away by their father on his semi-royal brood. Joan, the dowager Countess, fully supported by her son Richard, would yield nothing of her possessions, and when Earl Ralph married a daughter of the Nevilles' ancient rivals, the Percies, the general situation deteriorated to the point where physical violence was freely used by both sides.

Eventually, some sort of peace was patched up by arbitrators sent north by the Privy Council, but the enmity felt by the two sections of the family was now beyond mending. In 1440, the old Countess Joan died and left the castles at Middleham and Sheriff Hutton to Richard Neville, Earl of Salisbury, together with all the lands willed to her by her late husband. Thus, Salisbury became one of the greatest magnates in the land and a Lord who had served King and country well in warfare and negotiations equally, with both Scots and French. This work had brought him a seat on the Privy Council, which effectively ruled England during the minority of Henry VI, and Salisbury spent much of his time in London attending to the great affairs of state and working closely with Cardinal Beaufort, second son of the liaison between John of Gaunt and Katherine Swynford, who acted as First Minister of England.

The year before the death of the great Countess, Richard Beauchamp,

**Richard Neville, Earl of Warwick, the Kingmaker, as a "Weeper" figure
on the tomb of his father-in-law Richard Beauchamp**

(Geoffrey Wheeler)

Earl of Warwick, had died and was succeeded by his son, Henry who, the two fathers being lifelong friends, had been married young to Cecily Neville, named for her aunt [the Rose of Raby] and second daughter of Salisbury. And, while Henry of Warwick was affianced to Cecily, so his sister Anne was betrothed to the younger Richard Neville, in a dual coupling of the two families. Henry of Warwick was raised with Henry VI, who had been put into the Warwick household to ensure his proper upbringing in the ways of chivalry and kingship. The two Henrys were bosom friends and there could have been little doubt as to who would have become Henry's chief adviser when he took upon himself the rule of the kingdom.

Unhappily for Henry VI - and for England - Henry Beauchamp died at the age of 22, shortly after his King had created him Duke of Warwick, and the guidance of the young ruler passed to other more-partial and less-wise hands, while inheritance of the Earldom and all its broad acres passed to the four year old daughter of Warwick and Cecily Neville, who was a ward of William de la Pole, Earl of Suffolk and no friend of the Neville family. There can be little doubt that de la Pole would have arranged a 'suitable' marriage for his wealthy ward in short order to disqualify the potential claims of the heir presumptive, Richard Neville, Salisbury's eldest son. But again, a malign fate took a hand and the child, Anne, died three years after her father in June, 1449, her vast patrimony then passing jointly to her mother's brother, and his wife, another Anne Beauchamp, and aunt to the child.

The new Earl of Warwick (the title of Duke passed to another branch of the Beauchamps) was 20 when the second of the two unlooked-for deaths snuffed out the life which stood between him and the Premier Earldom of England and transformed his prospects. The younger Richard Neville now possessed wealth far greater than his father with broad estates, castles, villages and towns coming with his new titles, in the Midlands, Wales and most of the counties across the southern coast of England. The castle and town of Warwick were his, as were the Manors of Tamworth and Wychwood and even in the Borders were new possessions: the fortress and lands of Barnard Castle, closely adjacent to the Nevilles ancestral holdings.

It was the year 1449 when Richard Neville, proud grandson of Joan Beaufort and thereby great-great grandson of Edward III, attained his 21st year and assumed his new title and holdings. And, in the same year, the tide turned decisively in favour of the French, fighting to regain their lands in Normandy from the long-established English rule, and, within four years,

France again controlled not only Normandy, but the former possessions in Gascony, which the Plantagenets, 300 years earlier, had added to their new English Kingdom.

Of all the English conquests in France, by 1453 only Calais remained and England was filled with disgruntled archers, men-at-arms, and their Lords, who had lost pride and possessions and looked for redress on both counts from whomsoever had the obligation, or the ability, to pay. The settling time had come.

Warwick Castle from an Engraving by S & N Buck

(Geoffrey Wheeler)

CHAPTER THREE

"The Way to dusty death ...
(Macbeth)

In the August of 1453, Henry VI, King of England - and latterly of much of France - had one of the fits of acute melancholia which were to trouble him for much of his life and which made him totally incapable of governing his realm. The court party led by the Queen, Margaret of Anjou, and the Duke of Somerset, Edmund Beaufort, were quite happy to rule in his stead - there was a growing opinion abroad that they did this anyway through their control of the unhappy monarch - but the Privy Council and Parliament vested the temporary rule of the kingdom in the hands of Richard Plantagenet, Duke of York, brother-in-law to the Earl of Salisbury and uncle of the Earl of Warwick.

Old, grey Talbot, Earl of Shrewsbury and last of the English Paladins against the French, whose name had been used for decades by mothers in France to quieten querulous infants 'Lest Talbote come for you' had died at Castillon, in what was to prove his country's last defeat of the Hundred Years War, on July 17th. The shock wrought by the news of his death and the resultant, and imminent, loss of what remained of Gascony were blamed on Somerset and the Queen - the Frenchwoman - who were held to have sent the heroic Talbot to his death for want of men and supplies. Hence the preference for York as Protector during the King's illness, which was justified apparently when Bordeaux, the last bastion of Gascony, fell on October 10th, never to return to English rule.

The Duke of York summoned the first parliament after the defeat and it was noted that his nephew, Richard Neville, rode into London at the Duke's side and that they were shortly joined by the older Neville, Earl of Salisbury. All three brought strong contingents of well-equipped men-at-arms with them, matching the similar bands accompanying supporters of Somerset and Queen Margaret. However, there was no outright bickering between the two parties and Warwick, now a Privy Counsellor, and his father Salisbury, made Chancellor by York, helped the Protector to rule the Kingdom well and quietly during the King's madness.

A son had been born to the Queen on October 15th of the previous year and York, with the Nevilles, sat on the Commission which agreed the infant, Edward, be created Prince of Wales and acknowledged as heir to the throne, thus effectively displacing York himself from that role. Rumours were circulating that the new Prince was in truth a bastard sired by Somerset and that the King, when the babe was presented to him, declared he must have been conceived by the Holy Ghost, but these were disregarded by the Yorkist Lords. Apart from Somerset, who had been sent to the Tower to await trial for his shortcomings in supplying Talbot and for falsely accusing Richard of York of conspiracy to displace the King, no supporter of the Queen's court party suffered harm during the Protectorate. Indeed, York went to considerable lengths to mediate for peaceful settlement of a revived quarrel between the Nevilles and the Percies, in which he succeeded, but at the cost of incurring the enduring enmity of the Lords of Northumberland.

On the Feast of the Nativity, as suddenly as he had fallen sick, Henry VI recovered his wits and re-assumed the rule of his Kingdom. Immediately, the Queen called for the release of Somerset from his imprisonment and this being done, York and Salisbury were dismissed from their high office and returned to their estates, York to Sandal Castle near Wakefield and Salisbury to his great Keep at Middleham. Warwick, meantime, watched and waited from his own Earldom in the Midlands.

In May, 1455, the King summoned a Council which in turn summoned a Parliament to be held in Leicester later the same month, the main purpose of which was "to provide for the safety of the King's person against his enemies". The Duke of York and the Earls of Salisbury and Warwick were not amongst the magnates summoned to the Parliament, nor were any of the supporters of the House of York, leaving little doubt in the minds of the three chief players as to who were to be designated enemies of His Majesty and the kind of treatment that would be meted out to them shortly thereafter.

Accordingly, York gathered his men at Sandal, where Salisbury marched from Middleham to join with him and the two marched rapidly south, meeting with Warwick en route to London. By the 20th of May, the Yorkist force, by dint of rapid marching was 40 miles north of London at Royston in Hertfordshire and hoped to reach the capital in two days' time.

Meantime the King, escorted by Somerset, the Duke of Buckingham, Lord Clifford and the Earl of Northumberland, with their menies, had set out for Leicester, unaware that the Duke of York with his Neville allies was coming to meet with him and to demand the execution of Somerset and others "such as we will accuse". The King's party reached Watford on the 21st and rested there for the night; the Yorkists had moved on to Ware and the two forces were now only 20 miles apart with neither aware of the other's movements or even existence. However, this was soon remedied during the late evening, when York's scouts located the King's army and Somerset's men found the oncoming northern men encamped at Ware.

The next move for both sides was obvious. The gateway to London, St Albans, was equidistant from the two parties and the morning of May 22nd, 1455 dawned on a race by two armies to reach the town. York and Salisbury, swinging south of Hatfield and then pressing due west reached the Tonman Ditch, part of the ancient defences of St Albans about the middle of the morning, to find their way blocked by the moveable log barriers which the townspeople could swing across the ditch to block the road crossings. The King had reached the town before them and they could see the sun glinting on armour and spearpoints behind the barricades and hear the rumbling murmur of a strong force of men forming in divisions in Holywell and St Peter's Streets ready to react to any move on the part of their opponents.

Arms of the Cliffords.
The checks alternate in gold and blue,
the crossband is in red.

CHAPTER FOUR

"And more such days as these to us befall."
(Henry VI, Part 2)

Disappointed in their first design, the Duke of York and his Neville supporters spread their own force along the ditch facing the town and awaited developments. The scent of battle was in the air. When it came - if it came - none could foresee that it would be 30 years before the swords would be finally sheathed again. The Lords and Captains gave no immediate thought to the future, their minds were entirely set on immediate problems; and their men, likewise, were content for the moment to rest their tired bodies, to chat and joke, to relieve themselves, to eat what food they carried with them, and then to check their weapons, as they had done so many times in France in another place, another war. None knew - how could they - that here they would fight the first Battle of St Albans and with it, the Wars of the Roses - the great Civil War of England - would have begun.

At mid-morning, a parley was sounded from behind the barrier across Shropshire Lane, where King Henry's banner showed alongside the arms of Somerset, and the old Duke of Buckingham, Humphrey Stafford, who had grown grey in the service of Henry and his illustrious father, passed through the facing lines and was conducted to the group of Yorkist leaders. Richard Plantagenet, Duke of York, and second in line to the throne stood with his brother-in-law, Richard Neville, Earl of Salisbury and gave courteous welcome to the husband of Salisbury's sister, Anne.

Flanking the two leaders, watchful, silent, were the younger Richard Neville, now 27 years old and still unblooded in battle, and Sir Robert Ogle, Constable of Norham Castle, who had brought 600 of his hard-bitten troopers south with him from the Scottish Border country at Salisbury's call. Ogle and his men, vastly experienced in warfare through their part in the continual deadly bickering with the Scots, would play a key role in what was to come on that bright, early Summer's day in the twisting lanes of a small Hertfordshire town.

After the exchange of basic courtesies, Buckingham gave the Yorkists the commands from their King, namely that they should cease and desist from their rebellious behaviour and yield themselves immediately to his judgement. This, York and Salisbury were unwilling to do, instead, while protesting continuing loyalty to their sovereign Lord, they respectfully demanded that "such as we shall accuse" be handed over to them for their judgement. With this message, Buckingham returned to the King, who in a fit of unaccustomed rage, swore that he would "destroy these traitors, every mother's son, and they shall be hanged, drawn and quartered".

The lines had been finally drawn. On the one side, Somerset eager to advance his proximity to the throne by eliminating his hated rival, Richard of York, with Harry Percy of Northumberland who despised the upstart Nevilles and their high-born relative, and Thomas, Lord Clifford, another fierce, experienced fighter from the Borders, eager to show his family's continuing loyalty to the House of Lancaster. Opposed to them, Richard Plantagenet, Duke of York and held by some to be the true heir to the throne of England, married to Cecily Neville and thereby brother-in-law to Salisbury, who bore strongly his family's ancient grudge against the Percies, and uncle to Warwick, who had come off second best in a familial dispute with Edmund Beaufort, Duke of Somerset, over lands in South Wales and who had a long memory for inflicted injury. Whatever the outcome of the now inevitable fight, noble blood must flow freely in the settlement of so many old, festering scores.

At about noon, the King's forces, anticipating the usual continuing discussion between the two sides, were relaxing within the town and taking their mid-day meals. Fortunately their leaders had ensured that the barriers across the town ditch were fully manned, for before the hour struck, Salisbury on the left and York on the right attacked up the two main approach roads. The barriers halted their charge and the battle quickly moved towards stalemate with the Yorkists unable to force their way through into the streets of the town through the determined defence of Clifford against Salisbury and Somerset against York. Northumberland's men, set to guard Cock Lane, the approach from Hatfield, were not immediately involved in the battle, nor were Ogle and Warwick whose joint division was located between the two main Yorkist attacks.

Robert Ogle, veteran of many a bitter border-fight, had sent scouts to his front to find whether his and Warwick's men could make headway in support

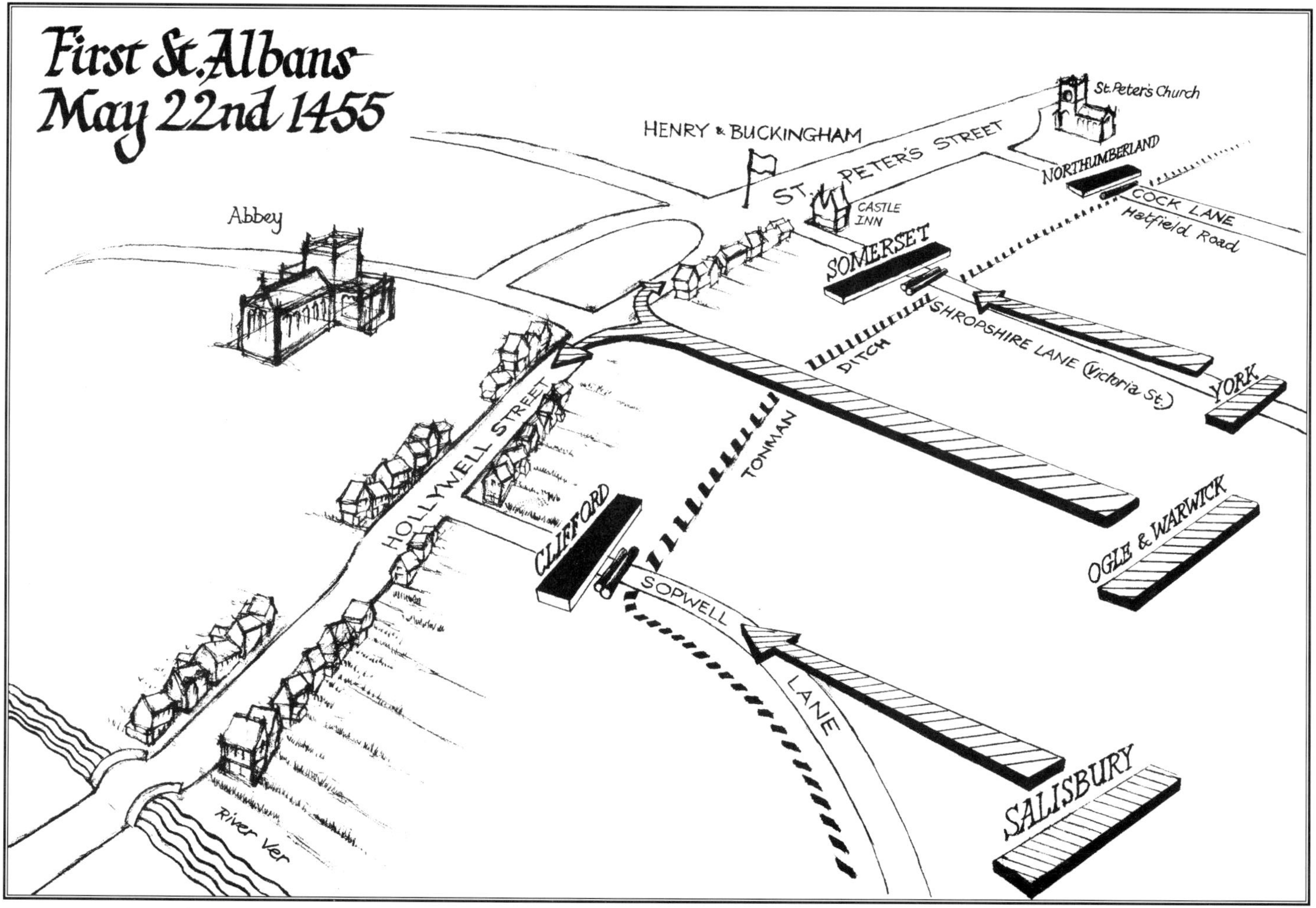
First St. Albans
May 22nd 1455
Abbey
HENRY & BUCKINGHAM
St. Peter's Church
ST. PETER'S STREET
CASTLE INN
NORTHUMBERLAND
COCK LANE
Hatfield Road
SOMERSET
SHROPSHIRE LANE (Victoria St.)
DITCH
YORK
TONMAN
HOLLYWELL STREET
CLIFFORD
OGLE & WARWICK
SOPWELL LANE
SALISBURY
River Ver

of their seniors and, when these patrols returned saying there was no opposing force in the gardens and allotments before them and it became more obvious that their other attacks were failing, Ogle and Richard Neville moved forward, unopposed, until they reached the backs of the houses facing into Holywell and St Peters Streets. Breaking through the frail walls, the column forced its way out into the town and debouched to right and left with great shouts of "A Warwick, A Warwick", taking the stalwart defenders of the barricades in the rear and flanking Northumberland's men who broke and fled out of the town.

Salisbury's and York's divisions forced their way through and over the dwindling resistance facing them and the main fighting was quickly ended, with the beaten men of Lancaster paying the usual heavy price of defeat. According to a close eye-witness, the Abbot of St Albans, John Whethamstede, "the whole street was full of dead corpses" and, among them - dead in the dusty streets - were found the stripped bodies of Henry Percy, second Earl of Northumberland, Lord Thomas Clifford, for whom a heavy blood-geld would be paid, and Edmund Beaufort, second Duke of Somerset, reputed lover of Queen Margaret, Chief Councillor to the King and no longer a remembered-thorn in the side of Richard Neville, Earl of Warwick.

The Duke of Buckingham had fared better - though his son and heir Humphrey, Earl of Stafford, was among the dead - having sat with the King in the Market Square throughout the fighting. Both were slightly wounded by arrows - Buckingham in the face, Henry in the neck - neither having taken the trouble to wear his casque, but the King was not too badly hurt to give gracious reception to the repentant York, Salisbury and Warwick, when they waited on him immediately and asked forgiveness for imperilling his royal life. Hardly surprisingly, Henry felt able to forgive the victors, who gathered their men and triumphantly marched out for London, taking the King with them and leaving the monks and townsfolk of St Albans to mend their houses and bury the dead.

The first blows of the Wars of the Roses had been struck - the first blood debts incurred - and the seedlings of the final destruction of the House of Plantagenet, which had ruled in England for near three hundred years, had taken firm hold in fertile soil.

CHAPTER FIVE

Alarums and Excursions.
(Kipling)

ith Somerset dead and the King in his control, York might have expected to resume his old power in the land, but this could not be while Henry's Queen, Margaret of Anjou, continuously devised ways to set the central authority at naught and schemed to resume her own place at Henry's side and her monopoly of the royal ear. She was helped by a general resentment among the English nobility towards the nouveaux-riches Nevilles who, despite their Beaufort descent, were regarded as nobodies from the north who had married well, and York sacrificed much of his basic popularity by forcing through the November 1455 Parliament a resumption of his Protectorship on what was seen as a pretext of restoring order in the West Country.

Nevertheless, the Neville family had gained quite handsomely from their part in the victory at St Albans. Salisbury had been appointed to a number of important Royal Stewardships - profitable offices under the crown - including those of the Duchy of Lancaster north of Trent, of Lancashire, and of Pickering in north Yorkshire. With his son, Warwick, he was continued in his duties as Warden of the West Marches on improved financial terms, and his brother William, Lord Fauconberg, gained a half share in the office of Constable of Windsor Castle. Warwick's younger brother, George, was granted the Bishopric of Exeter and for Richard Neville, Earl of Warwick, himself, the Captaincy of Calais, command of England's most important fortress and garrison beyond the shores of Britain.

By the following February, the King - who had suffered another attack of melancholia in the aftermath of St Albans - had recovered his wits sufficiently to attend the new Parliament in person and relieve York of his office. The Queen meantime had taken her son, Edward, Prince of Wales, to the old Lancastrian heartland in the west and there, progressively joined by adherents of the Court Party, her power waxed steadily ever-stronger. Soon she would be in a position to challenge York and the Nevilles again for the right to rule

England and as Summer drew to its close, she was able to arrange for the King to be removed to Coventry.

Moving quickly to build on her advantage, Margaret called a meeting of the Great Council in the King's name, with York and Warwick included in the summons. Following his removal from the duties of Protector, York had moved north again to his estates around Sandal and Salisbury had gone with him, moving on to Middleham and Raby where he occupied himself with the management of his private affairs, as did Warwick from his great castle in the Midlands. They obeyed the King's call and found themselves in a minority of two at the Council table where the King, ostensibly presiding, gave royal authority to a stern lecture delivered by Buckingham to the recalcitrant pair, who were then obliged to swear and seal their submission and guaranty of future good and dutiful conduct, before being permitted to take their leave.

Still worse might have befallen Plantagenet and Neville but Humphrey Stafford, although he had lost his son at St Albans, was by marriage brother-in-law to York and uncle to Warwick, and he warned them of an impending ambush by the new Duke of Somerset and Lord John Clifford, who aimed at avenging the deaths of their respective parents in the battle. Gratefully, the two slipped away from Coventry, York to his estates in the Welsh Marches and Warwick, with his wife and two small daughters, to take up his post as Captain of Calais which the Court had left to him as the furthest Royal estate from the heart of England's governance. This would prove to be a major error of judgement, for them and for England.

Calais, England's last foothold on the mainland of Europe and a tiny proportion of its former French dominions, was still a substantial fortress some 20 square miles in all, with powerful fortifications and guarded by castles at Hammes and Guisnes. With its sister-ports across the Channel, the command of Calais enabled its English masters to cut sea-borne trade between the north and south of the Continent at will and its strategic location was a factor Warwick was to exploit to great effect during his Captaincy.

Similarly on the land, Calais was well located to be involved in - or to stand aside from - the constant arguments between the Dukes of Burgundy, who, in addition to their great holding in central and southern France counted Holland and Flanders as their estates, and their feudal suzerain, the King of

France. Since Queen Margaret and her Court Party favoured the French connection, it was natural for York and the Nevilles to lean towards the Burgundian side and to agree on mutual support as and when the enemy to the south was stirring.

Richard Neville, Earl of Warwick, arrived in Calais in the late Autumn of 1456, to find the great English fortress in the early stages of military decay. Wages for the garrisons were badly in arrears and essential repair and upkeep of the fortifications had been sadly neglected, due to lack of funding from England, where the Royal Treasury was diverted regularly for the personal benefit of the Queen and her favourites. The fleet normally based at the port for defence and offence was similarly run-down and the Channel was rife with piracy and increasingly dominated by French ships of war. Thus far, the King of France had not been able to move aggressively on land against Calais because the Duke of Burgundy would not permit the French army to move across Burgundian soil, but Warwick, now 28 and rapidly maturing as a statesman of some quality, realised that the Port must act quickly and strongly in its own defence if its freedom from French rule were to be maintained.

Accordingly Richard Neville - impatient of further pointless delay involved in waiting for funding from the Treasury - used his own vast resources to pay his garrisons, improve their weaponry, repair his walls, and to recruit new men-at-arms and, equally important, skilled seamen to man a larger fleet. He sailed himself with master mariners to learn their craft and seemed to find the manoeuvre and mathematics involved in sea-warfare more to his liking than the grim. toe-to-toe slogging matches to which land-battles were all too often reduced. The Earl of Warwick took to sea fighting like the proverbial duck to water.

In light of his new-found fascination with the seas, and the need to find additional funds for securing Calais, Warwick also took to piracy. The opportunity to take this course was thrust upon him by the action of the French fleet under Piers de Brezé, Seneschal of Normandy, who, sensing the weakness of the English forces available to oppose a major incursion and encouraged by Margaret of Anjou - an old family friend - to damage the standing of York and the Nevilles in the land, made a great raid, in the late Summer of 1457 on the Kentish port of Sandwich. Here, the French killed bailiffs, men of the cloth and of quality, looted raped and burned and withdrew unscathed to their home ports again. The humiliation, as much as the material loss, hurt English pride and the involvement of the Queen and the supineness of the Home Fleet of which the Duke of Exeter, leading Lancastrian and Lord High Admiral, was nominally the leader did much harm to the cause of the Court, particularly in Kent which became a hotbed of Yorkist support for many years thereafter.

In October, Warwick found himself granted the grand title of Keeper of the Seas by the King's Council, together with a certain amount of financial support towards expansion of his fleet. In May the following year, his force had grown sufficiently to risk an attack on a well-protected Spanish convoy - the Spanish were allied to the French - and after a six-hour engagement succeeded in sinking two and capturing six of the enemy. Shortly thereafter, a fleet of merchantmen owned by the Hanseatic League passed up the Channel carrying a good cargo for their home ports and failed to pay proper respect, by dipping their ensigns, to the Captain of Calais. Without more ado, Warwick put to sea and captured virtually all the vessels, confiscating their burdens.

By the Summer of 1459, Richard Neville and his privateering navy were the dominant force in the Channel and added further laurels with the defeat and capture of a mixed fleet comprising two Genoese carracks escorted by three Spanish men-of-war, which victory paid the winners handsomely in spices and silks sold in the markets of London and Calais. To the English, still bitter about their final defeat in the French wars, it seemed that in Warwick, they had found a new champion, who would restore their lost fortunes and lead them on to rule still greater Empires than that they had lost across the Channel.

Warwick's reputation as a great leader of men had spread further afield than England and, in the same year, he was invited to meet the great Duke of Burgundy, Philip, who went out of his way to impress Richard Neville with his wealth, culture and power. The two noblemen were equally impressed, one with the other, and Warwick also met with Louis the Dauphin (later Louis XI, the Spider King) who was in sanctuary at the Burgundian court following one of his regular furious quarrels with his father. Louis, much less magnificent in appearance than his host, was much more subtle in scheming, in shaping strategies and constructing plots to gain his ends. In short, despite a tendency to epileptic fits and the illogical behavioural patterns which sometimes go with them, Louis the master strategist was a man more to Warwick's liking than the magnificent Philip could ever be and the close association between the two would continue and strengthen, until Richard Neville paid for it with his life.

CHAPTER SIX

Peace and Prayer and Return to War.

During 1458, Warwick had returned to England on two occasions, first, at the behest of the Council, to take part in a formal and public reconciliation with the leaders of Lancaster. Under the terms of this arrangement, York, Salisbury and Warwick agreed to pay £ 45 per year in perpetuity to St Albans Abbey so that masses might be sung for the souls of Somerset, Clifford, Northumberland, Stafford and other gentlemen who had died in the battle.

Further, indemnities were paid by York to the widow and heir of Somerset and by Warwick to the Clifford family, though since these were paid by transfer of i.o.u.'s for sums owed by the Royal Treasury to the two Yorkists for expenses they had incurred in the national behalf in France and Ireland, the real value of the assignments was doubtful to say the least. And, to complete the charade of goodwill, the citizens of London were treated to the unlikely spectacle of the parties most closely involved, led by the King, processing to St Paul's two by two - York and Somerset, Salisbury with Wiltshire, and Warwick with Clifford, to give thanks for their rapprochement.

Warwick's second return visit some seven months later was to answer charges made by the Queen relating to his attack on the Hanseatic ships - vessels and cargoes being "owned by persons under the King's friendship". On arrival, he saw that there were no friends of York called to the Council and his men were jostled in the antechamber to an extent that Warwick felt discretion to be the better part of valour and he and his followers left Westminster abruptly. He returned to Calais without more ado, pausing only to send news to York and his father of what had occurred and warning that they would doubtless be the next targets of the Queen's malice. Safely back in his French fortress, he awaited developments and the call from his kinfolk which he knew must come ere too long.

While Warwick had been gaining renown in Calais and the English Channel, his father had been living quietly, but watchfully, and guarding his chief inheritance in north Yorkshire from the great Keep of Middleham. Initially, all had gone well but by the Spring of 1457, problems had begun to accumulate. In March, Henry Percy finally succeeded to his Earldom of Northumberland almost two years after his father's death at St Albans, during which time he had been kept busy by Scottish incursions in the East March. Late the previous year, the Scots had agreed to a renewal of the truce and, with his formal accession to the title, Percy was reappointed Warden for a further 10 years, and his brother Sir Ralph Percy was made Constable of Dunstanburg Castle.

Simultaneously with Sir Ralph's appointment, Humphrey Neville of the rival Westmorland branch of the family was awarded the Stewardship of Richmondshire, and made Constable of Richmond Castle during the minority of Henry Tudor, son of the King's late half-brother, both posts being in the keeping of a nominee of Richard Neville. And, in the July of the year came a further and more serious blow to Salisbury's dominance in the North with the death of his younger brother, Robert, for twenty years the all-powerful Bishop of Durham. His replacement, Laurence Booth, had long served Queen Margaret and his appearance in Durham quickly led on to cancellation of annuities and offices granted by Robert Neville to members and adherents of his own family. The hold of the Nevilles of Middleham on the lands south of the Border was beginning to crumble.

The Duke of York, relying on his brother-in-law to watch the north, had lodged mainly in his stronghold at Ludlow from whence he kept a close eye on the activities of Queen Margaret as she persuaded the Lords and Gentlemen of the Midlands and the Northwest to the cause of her husband and, increasingly, of her son, Edward Prince of Wales. The Prince's personal livery combined an ostrich feather and a swan and Margaret used the 'Livery of the Swan' as a new focal point to draw knights and squires to swear loyalty to her son.

The Queen's faction, led by the Duke of Somerset and Lord Clifford, gathered strength rapidly through the early Summer of 1459 and bands of Lancastrian horse raided and robbed the properties of their rivals around Warwick and in Yorkshire. By August, Richard Plantagenet, learning that a veritable army was now in being and moving steadily towards his Keep at Ludlow, where he had taken his wife and family for their greater protection, sent urgently to Salisbury at Middleham and Warwick in Calais to come and join him. The Nevilles responded that they would join him at Ludlow without delay and with all the strength they could safely muster from their garrisons.

Warwick crossed the Channel in mid-September, passed through Kent and London and moved north towards his estates in the Midlands. Salisbury left Middleham, accompanied by his second and third sons Thomas and John, on or about the 15th of the month and by Sunday the 23rd - the Feast of St Matthew - was leading his force of some 5,000 men-at-arms and mounted archers through Newcastle-under-Lyme, southwest towards Market Drayton en route for Ludlow. Reports from his scouts indicated that a very large and hostile force was moving directly towards him from Drayton, but Neville knew York's need for the reinforcement he was leading was desperate and he pressed on behind a strengthened screen of scouts.

Salisbury's force passed through a thickly forested area, Rowney Wood, and emerged into open country beyond, where their road swung leftwards and down into a narrow, steep-sided vale, through which flowed the Wemberton Brook. After a shallow ford-crossing, the road onwards led up the slope on the other side topped by a ridge along which Salisbury saw armoured cavalry deploying rapidly into line to prevent his further advance. Four years and more after the bloody brawl in the dusty, crowded streets of St Albans, Lancaster would meet York again, this time in the open fields of Staffordshire at Blore Heath.

The Lancastrian force of some 6,000 well-equipped cavalry was led by James Touchet, Lord Audley and Lord John Dudley and had been moving south from Cheshire to join King Henry's army near Coleshill. They were met by Queen Margaret near Stafford and ordered by her to intercept the approaching Salisbury, prevent his junction with York at Ludlow, and if possible arrest or kill him. Audley and Dudley, like most of the senior English nobility, had experience of leading men into battle from the French Wars and on seeing the head of Salisbury's column emerging from Rowney Wood a mile away across the Heath, decided to keep the advantage of their high ground along the ridge, moving to form their men up in two continuous divisions across the Yorkist line of advance. Audley, on the right, had a hedged lane to his front along which his men formed while Dudley's line on the opposite flank was protected by a fold in the ground directly before them. Each division had a ford over the Wemberton to their front, Audley's taking the road to Newcastle along which Salisbury had advanced, and Dudley's for

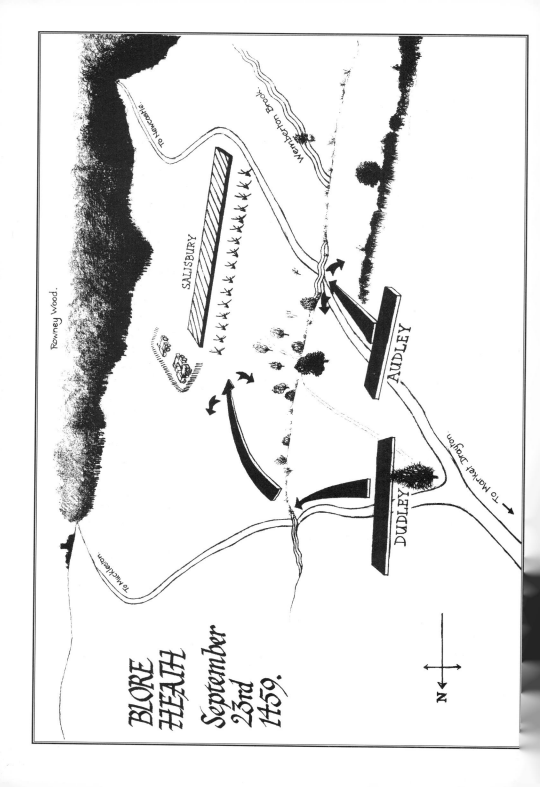

BLORE HEATH
September 23rd 1459.

SALISBURY

AUDLEY

DUDLEY

Rowney Wood.

Wemberton Brook.

To Newcastle

To Market Drayton

To Mucklestone

N

the track to the village of Muckleston. In this naturally strong defensive/offensive position, the Lancastrians settled and awaited Salisbury's move.

Richard Neville, Earl of Salisbury, was nearly 60 years old, a ripe age for his times; he had served in the French Wars, but gathered still more experience in constant fighting with the Scots on and over the Border. The prime lesson he had learned in both theatres was caution and seeing the forces of Lancaster forming into line across the Heath he ordered his own men to parallel them, placing dismounted men-at-arms in the front ranks, and his more mobile archers in the rear whence they could move quickly to support their heavily armoured comrades in attack or defence. His left flank extended towards the brook, where marshy ground protected it and his open right wing he covered by laagering his baggage wagons there, a tactic often used in France. Then, his line formed, Salisbury too stood and awaited developments.

As often happened on such occasions, there was much issuing of challenges and shouts of defiance from both sides. The mounted Lancastrians in particular, made great show of trotting their chargers to and fro, making them kick and plunge as their riders flaunted their banners towards the waiting Yorkist lines. About one hour after noon, the temper of Audley's wing had risen to fever pitch, there was considerable stirring within their ranks and the volume of shouts and curses redoubled. Salisbury, watching for any sign of developing attack across the mile separating the lines, interpreted the growing movement along Audley's division as preliminary to a mounted charge and, as Henry V had done at Agincourt, ordered his archers to the front to deal with the impending onslaught of mounted knights.

Audley, likewise viewing his enemy from long distance, saw Salisbury's line of armoured men-at-arms withdrawing as though preparatory to a general retreat into the nearby woods immediately to his rear and seized this seeming opportunity. Sending to Dudley to follow his example as quickly as might be, Audley advanced his own banner and led his division in a furious charge down the slope towards the ford - and the waiting line of archers. As the charge lost its first impetus, slowing to cross the Wemberton, Salisbury ordered his archers to shoot and shelf after shelf of arrows flew into the milling mass of horses and men with predictable results. Hopelessly tangled, the Lancastrian line twisted and turned on itself and dissolved. Audley, his first charger killed, remounted and tried to lead his men back to the charge, but when he was struck by an arrow and killed, his remaining followers fled.

Meantime, Dudley had received Audley's message and had started his division down towards the Wemberton in support of the first attack, but reached the brook only in time to see the defeat of their comrades and their rapid withdrawal back up the slope out of arrow range and back over the ridge they had left less than an hour before. Salisbury's archers switched their fire to the new target, but Dudley dismounted his men and led them in more orthodox fashion towards the Yorkist centre, hoping that Audley's wing would rally to his support. Unfortunately for him, his erstwhile comrades had had enough of this fight and concentrated all their efforts on escape, except for one group of some 500 who changed their previous warcries to "A Neville, A Neville" and joined Salisbury's ranks. With Dudley wounded and captured, the discipline of Lancaster's army collapsed and the men of York enjoyed a pursuit lasting until dark, raising the eventual death-toll to 2,000 with many Swan Liverymen numbered amongst them, including five newly-dubbed Knights of the Order.

Richard Neville, a famous victory under his belt, his losses minimal, reformed his column as the evening shadows lengthened and resumed his march towards Shrewsbury and Ludlow. No forces of Lancaster strong enough to oppose his advance now stood between him and his goal, but, to the east of York's massive Keep, a great army loyal to King Henry and led by Somerset and Clifford was assembled and now moved steadily towards a final confrontation with the great rebels against the King's majesty.

Sheriff Hutton Castle from an Engraving by S & N Buck
(Geoffrey Wheeler)

CHAPTER SEVEN

Defeat and Flight.

hile his father was gaining victory at Blore Heath, Richard Neville, Earl of Warwick, Captain of Calais, leaving his uncle, William Neville, Lord Fauconberg in command had crossed the Channel with 600 of his garrison. He marched quickly through Kent to London, where his forces were welcomed by the City Fathers and where Warwick took the opportunity to issue a proclamation of loyalty to King Henry saying he, his father and the Duke of York his uncle, had taken up arms only to defend themselves and their lands, and praying that His Majesty would heed their just demands.

He left London on September 21st and marched rapidly north to his castle at Warwick, where he found much evidence of depredation by Lancastrian troops, then moved on westwards towards the Yorkist rendezvous at Ludlow. As he passed by Coleshill in the Midlands, Warwick narrowly avoided clashing with a much superior force led by Henry Beaufort, Duke of Somerset, which was marching to join the King's army, but escaped without hurt to reunite with the Yorkist forces at Ludlow.

There, in addition to his father and uncle, he found Edward, Earl of March, York's eldest son, with his brother Edmund, Earl of Rutland; the two young men were aged 17 and 16 respectively and eager for their first taste of battle. The older men, however, were not happy with the reports their scouts were bringing in, which indicated that the King's army was much larger than their own and, although they waited in Ludlow for two weeks in the hope of further reinforcement, the opposing force grew even more quickly, leaving York and the Nevilles well outnumbered.

As the Royal army approached, York, unwilling to be besieged in Ludlow Castle, where he could neither lodge nor feed the host he had assembled, moved out into the field and dug earthworks to the south of the town, blocking the road from Leominster up which the King's army was advancing. To temporise, he and the Nevilles had sent letters to the King protesting their loyalty and complaining of the slanders being made against them by the Court party. At the prompting of his wife and Somerset, Henry replied that he would give them grace of their lives and goods if they surrendered to him, excepting only such persons as had been concerned in the death of Lord Audley. The implicit threat in this response to all the leaders of the Yorkist faction was clear and, outnumbered as they were, there seemed no other option but to man their earthworks and await events.

Somerset, more subtle than his father before him, had sent a further letter into the Yorkist lines by covert means and addressed to one Andrew Trollope, a captain of the Calais garrison who had accompanied Warwick across the Channel as his senior subordinate. Trollope's sympathies were with the Lancastrians and Somerset offered full pardon to him and his men if they would desert Neville's cause and come over to the King's side. On the night of October 13th, 1459, Trollope with his 600 men-at-arms and archers slipped quietly away from their earthworks and moved silently across the muddy field before them to be met and greeted warmly by Somerset and the forces opposite.

The defection of the Calais men was discovered shortly before dawn and this significant weakening of their line and the accompanying loss of morale among their other men left the Nevilles and York, as leaders of a dwindling rebel army, with no option but to flee for their lives. They had no illusions as to the kind of justice which would be meted out to them by Margaret of Anjou and their Beaufort cousins and preferred immediate flight with a view to returning in better times. York with his second son, Rutland, rode hard for the west coast and made for his estates in Ireland, where his previous, happy tenure as Henry's Lieutenant assured him of a warm welcome and sure sanctuary.

The two Nevilles, with Edward of March and accompanied by Sir John Dynham, made for the southwest where, on the north Devon coast, they were able to scrape sufficient funds together for Dynham to buy a sea-worthy boat in which, according to legend, Warwick navigated them to Guernsey and thence to Calais, which Fauconberg continued to hold securely for the Yorkists.

When Somerset and his men had passed through the empty earthworks the next morning and entered the town, the only prisoners left for them to take were Cecily Neville, Duchess of York and her two younger sons, George and Richard. However, they were arrested and sent for safe-keeping to Coventry Castle, where at a Parliament in the following month, York and the Nevilles were jointly and severally attainted as traitors and all their goods were declared forfeit to the crown. Cecily and her boys were committed to the custody of her elder sister, Anne, Duchess of Buckingham, and the King allotted 1,000 marks a year for their upkeep from his Treasury, which had been - briefly - replenished by the wealth of the erstwhile rebels.

All the lands of the rebels reverted to the Crown and their various Offices were allotted to Lords loyal to the House of Lancaster. The important Wardenship of the West March went to Lord Clifford, and Viscount Beaumont took Salisbury's post as Chief Steward of the Duchy of Lancaster in the north. Lord John Neville, brother of the Earl of Westmorland, became Constable and Steward of Sheriff Hutton, and another brother, Humphrey, was made Parker of Caplebank in Middleham. Lord Fitzhugh was installed as Steward of Middleham and Richmond and, from the Royal Household, William Branklow became Parker of the Great Park of Middleham.

Income from Salisbury's lands in Worton and Wensleydale went, among others, to John Neville and Lord Scrope of Masham, but the bulk of these revenues were reserved for Henry Percy, Earl of Northumberland, to set against his arrears for his time in office as Captain of Berwick. In Durham, the Queen's nominee, Bishop Laurence Booth, completed the despoiling of the Nevilles by confiscating Warwick's lordship of Barnard Castle and installing his own men in the key roles of Receiver and Constable and Master Forester of Teesdale.

From the wealthiest Lords in the Kingdom, Salisbury and Warwick were reduced to paupers and the future for them and their kin was bleak indeed. Unless the world could be turned upside down again by the strength of their swords.

Prior to the Coventry parliament, the King had appointed Henry Beaufort, Duke of Somerset, to be Captain of Calais and he lost little time in moving south to Sandwich and assembling a small fleet to escort him across the Channel to assume his office. By a trick of the wind, the fugitives' boat had reached Calais harbour a day or two before Somerset could cross and when the Duke finally attempted to enter the port he was met with cannonades from the artillery and volleys from hand-cannon and archers.

Seeing the Neville banners displayed on the fortifications, the would-be Captain was left in no further doubt as to the location of the rebel Lords - a question which had been puzzling the party of Lancaster, since the successful evasion at Ludlow. With Trollope and his men from the Calais garrison, which formed the main part of his escort, Somerset moved along the coast to the secondary fortress of Guisnes where he was able to land but had to watch his fleet swept away by a sudden storm from which the vessels had to run for shelter into Calais harbour. There, under the great guns of the port, they had no option but to surrender and the supplies of arms and stores they had brought with them were welcome reinforcement for the three Earls.

For some time, Somerset and Trollope were unable to trouble the Nevilles unduly, but once contacts had been established with the French court, the Lancastrians were able to re-equip their force and through the last two months of the year there was constant bickering between Guisnes and Calais. Towards Christmas, Warwick learned that Queen Margaret had managed to scrape together reinforcements for Somerset and these troops, under the leadership of Lord Rivers and his son, Sir Anthony Woodville, would cross to Guisnes before long. To pre-empt this attack, Warwick sent his two best sea-captains, Sir John Dynham and Sir John Wenlock, with what vessels he could muster to make a surprise attack on Sandwich where the Woodvilles were assembling. This raid was entirely successful and Dynham and Wenlock returned, bringing the main vessels as prizes into Calais and, with them, Rivers and Woodville who had been captured aboard their flagship.

To maximise the propaganda value of their triumph, the Earls staged an immediate public examination of the Woodvilles in which Salisbury and Warwick verbally attacked the hapless pair as common men whose family had achieved what little distinction they had through Rivers' marriage to Jaquetta, widow of the Duke of Bedford, Henry V's brother. While this was perfectly true, the irony of such statements, coming from two men who had gained their own Earldoms by marriage and whose blood-royal was via the bastard Beaufort line, may not entirely have escaped Rivers. More cutting perhaps was the following, similar tirade from Edward of March, whose claim to royal blood at least, was perfectly legitimate.

Their public abasement over, the two Lancastrians were - no doubt uncomfortably - lodged in the fortress of Calais and their captors celebrated Christmas secure from outside attack and well-supplied. Their happy situation continued into the new year and, in March, news arrived from Ireland that

Richard of York had succeeded in gathering a strong force and was expected to return to England before the year was out. Warwick immediately put to sea and sailed through some stormy weather to Dublin, where he conferred with the Yorkist leader and with him worked out detailed plans for a dual invasion in the Summer or early Autumn of 1460.

Towards the end of May, Warwick set out for Calais taking with him his mother who had fled to sanctuary with York after being attainted at Coventry, and brushing aside a feeble attempt by the Duke of Exeter, Lord High Admiral, to intercept his fleet off the Cornish coast, Richard Neville returned in triumph to Calais. There he restored his mother to her husband's tender care and immediately set on foot preparations for the return to England in which his father, uncle and cousin enthusiastically joined.

Garter Stall Plate of William Neville, Lord Fauconberg.

(St George's Chapel, Windsor)

45

CHAPTER EIGHT

"We returned to our places, these Kingdoms
But no longer at ease here in the old dispensation..."
(T.S. Eliot)

On the 27th of June, Richard Neville, Earl of Salisbury with his brother William, Lord Fauconberg, and his son the Earl of Warwick, his nephew the Earl of March, their fighting captains and an army of 2,000 crossed from Calais to Sandwich, where they proclaimed that they were loyal subjects of His Majesty, King Henry VI, and came back only to claim their own. Two days prior to the landing, Sir John Dynham had been sent by Warwick to clear a small Lancastrian garrison out of the port and this he had quickly achieved, sending the garrison's commander, Osbert Mundeford, who had been with Warwick and Trollope at Ludford Bridge, back to Calais for judgement. This he had, and speedily, Warwick seeing him beheaded in the square at Calais as he embarked for Sandwich.

The returning Earls were met by Thomas Bourchier, Archbishop of Canterbury, whose family were related to the House of York by marriage, and many hundreds of excited townspeople. They set out immediately for Canterbury to pray at the tomb of St Thomas a Becket and moved on towards London, their force growing stronger by the hour as they were joined by Kentish men and Men of Kent who, like much of England, were weary of the misrule of Lancaster and were, traditionally, ever-eager to join in potentially profitable forays to London. By July 1st, the Yorkist force, now many thousands strong, encamped at Blackheath, whence the following morning their leaders were escorted across the bridge by the City Fathers and the citizens of the capital into the seat of England's governance.

The swift movement of the Nevilles and the absence of any organised opposition, with the leaders of the Court Party in Coventry waiting on the King and Queen, or occupying themselves on their estates, had given the Yorkists quick and easy success. But Warwick, now emerging as the master-planner of his faction, was not prepared to sit on his gains and await events, He realised the Queen would be swift to react once news of events had reached Coventry and on July 3rd the advance guard of the Yorkist army moved north out of London led by the battle-hardened Fauconberg. The following morning, leaving a strong division commanded by Salisbury with Sir John Wenlock as his Lieutenant to watch the Lancastrian garrison commanded by Lord Scales which had locked itself within the Tower's walls, Warwick, with Edward of March and 4,000 well-mounted men-at-arms, followed his advance guard north towards Coventry.

King Henry was already moving south with a strong army led by his old general, and fellow-spectator at St Albans, Humphrey Stafford, first Duke of Buckingham, and had reached Northampton on July 8th. Here they were advised of the approach of Warwick's army, and being strong in artillery which made movement progressively difficult in an exceptionally wet English Summer, decided to build earthworks just to the south of the town, with the River Nene protecting the flanks and rear of their horseshoe entrenchment. Here they would await Warwick's attack, confident in the strength of their position and the power of their artillery.

On July 9th, Warwick's force reached Towcester and rejoined the advance guard led by Fauconberg, who told him of the King's arrival in Northampton and his preparations for battle south of the river. The Yorkists advanced to Hunsbury Hill, making camp there for the night and the following morning the two Nevilles, Warwick and Fauconberg, with Edward of March surveyed the King's position. This looked formidable, the earthworks being supported by a trench and timber spikes to the front, and embrasured at regular intervals with great guns set within these gaps.

On closer examination, however, the Yorkist leaders could see that much of the ground was waterlogged, thanks to the incessant rain, and the cannon were lying in pools of mud which would almost certainly render them useless in repelling any onslaught. On the other hand, the approaches to the fortifications were equally slippery with mud and puddles which must hamper the approach of heavily armoured infantry, and the best immediate prospect seemed to be the traditional approach through a parley between the two sides.

Warwick sent a group of high Churchmen, led by the Bishop of Salisbury, to request an audience with the King in which Warwick could state the case of himself and his family and ask for reinstatement in their places. When this was unsuccessful, the Archbishop of Canterbury accompanied by the Papal Legate, Francesco Coppini, whom the Pope had sent to England to try to reconcile the factions, made a similar effort and failed even more abysmally.

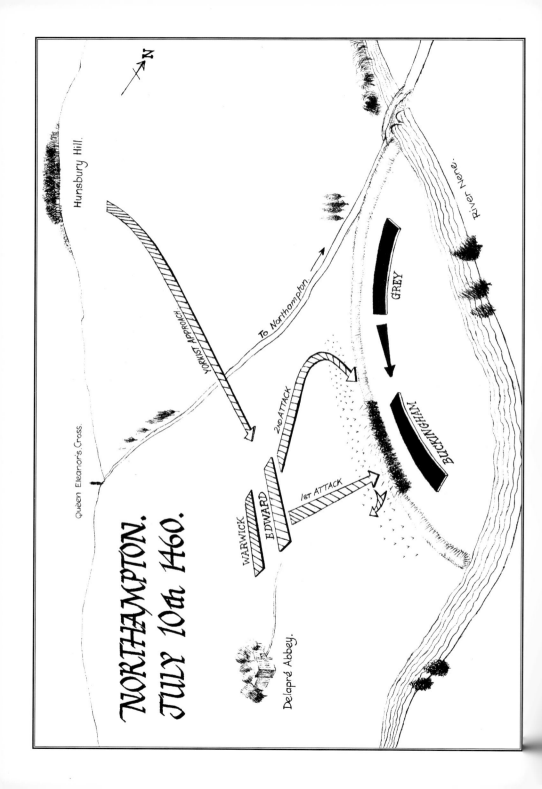

NORTHAMPTON.
JULY 10th 1460.

N

Hunsbury Hill.

River Nene.

Queen Eleanor's Cross.

To Northampton.

YORKIST APPROACH

GREY

BUCKINGHAM

2ND ATTACK

WARWICK

EDWARD

1ST ATTACK

Delapré Abbey.

Buckingham, noting the prelates' armed bodyguard, asked how they could require converse with His Majesty as men of God and peace, while bringing armed men into the Royal presence. The tart rejoinder from the Yorkist Archbishop was to the effect that even men of God had cause to fear the armed might of Lords like Buckingham and this ended negotiations. The Duke repeated his earlier threat that if Richard Neville approached the King he should die and Warwick responded that he would speak with His Majesty at two o clock of the afternoon, or die for it. And the two sides prepared themselves for battle.

Promptly at two in the afternoon the Yorkist army began its attack on the King's fortifications. They advanced in two divisions, one behind the other, with the vanward led by Edward of March, eager for his first battle-blooding, and the vastly more experienced Fauconberg who could restrain or support his younger companion as necessary. The rearguard and reserve was led by Warwick in his role as commanding general. The King's army, likewise. divided into two divisions manning their works side by side with a mobile screen of archers ready to assist on either flank. The left division was commanded by Buckingham himself, assisted by Thomas, Lord Egremont, brother to the Earl of Northumberland and by Lord Beaumont, while the right was led by Reginald Grey, Lord of Ruthyn.

Initially, the Yorkist attack was directed towards the King's left flank, where the ground seemed a little better, but this optimism was quickly disproved as the heavily weighted men found themselves struggling to make progress through mud so thick as to be little better than marshland. Fortunately for the slowly advancing Yorkists, their earlier assumptions on the uselessness of the cannons was quickly proved correct and the great guns played little or no part in the fight, but shelfs of arrows from the King's bowmen stung and wounded and killed until the line fell back in disarray, followed by the hoots and insults of their triumphant foes.

Angered by their losses and the scornful shouts of their enemy and pushed and shoved into some kind of order by their captains, the division turned again to attack, this time making for the other flank guarded by Grey of Ruthyn. With less opposition from the archers this time, Edward was able to lead the line up to the barricade lined by Grey's men who, with their leader, emulated Trollope at Ludford Bridge and switched sides, pulling down obstructions and joining the Yorkists in their assault on the, now, open flank of Buckingham's line.

The end was inevitable; the King's loyal troops broke and ran and many of them drowned in the River Nene which, only hours before, had seemed their sure protection against attack from the rear. King Henry suffered no harm in this fight, and accepted the humble submission of Warwick, Edward and Fauconberg as his most loyal and obedient subjects. Less fortunate were Humphrey Stafford, first Duke of Buckingham, Talbot, Earl of Shrewsbury, Percy, Lord Egremont, and John, Viscount Beaumont, who with many knights and squires lay dead on the field.

In triumph, Richard Neville led his victorious army back to London taking his sovereign Lord with him in close custody for his better protection. Arrived, Warwick lost no time in installing his family and allies in the key offices of the kingdom. His brother George, Bishop of Exeter, became Chancellor; Bourchier, brother to the Archbishop, was reinstalled as Treasurer; Laurence Booth the troublesome Bishop of Durham lost his office as Privy seal, and Edward of March and John Wenlock became members of the King's Council, of which Salisbury - again Chamberlain to the King - was absolute governor.

Away from London, however, the triumph of Yorkist arms at Northampton was largely ignored. At Middleham there was some progress towards the restoration of Salisbury's rights of Lordship, but Henry Percy of Northumberland repeatedly neglected to restore lordship of Wressle and Pontefract to their former owner and had arranged for one of the messengers bearing such Royal commands to be killed. Lord Clifford, wrathful and vengeful as ever over his father's death at St Albans, did nothing when, on October 8th, the King's command to clear Penrith of 'evil-doers' and hand the town back to Salisbury, was sent to him, and Lords Scrope, Dacre and Neville - Lancastrians all - likewise ignored repeated requests for support to be rendered to the senior Richard Neville. Indeed, all the Lancastrian nobility of northern England joined together in a veritable orgy of looting, rapine and destruction of lands and property belonging to Salisbury and to York.

In light of the increasing need for firm, prompt, legislative action to curb Northumberland, Clifford and their allies, and thereby correct the anarchy reigning across northern England, Warwick had called a Parliament for October 7th and sent urgently to his uncle that he should return from Dublin to reclaim his Duchy and lead Lords and Commons into courses aimed at re-establishing the rule of Law. Heeding this plea, and mindful of the reports of damage being done to his own, restored estates, the head of the House of

Plantagenet of York re-entered London on October 10th 1460 to great public acclamation amid scenes of considerable pomp and pageantry.

It was four months after the victory of his forces at Northampton and Richard Plantagenet, Duke of York, Lord Protector of England, life-long friend of the Nevilles and husband of Cecily Neville, the Rose of Raby, had little more than two months of life left to him.

Garter Stall Plate of Richard Neville, Earl of Salisbury.

(St George's Chapel, Windsor)

CHAPTER NINE

The Man who would be King.
(Kipling.)

During his year-long exile in Ireland, Richard of York had given deep thought to the course of events over the previous ten years. His inescapable conclusion was that he would never be able to enjoy peacefully his wealth, his estates and his family so long as Margaret of Anjou and her allies the Beauforts were able to manipulate the governance of England through their unbreakable hold on the King. It followed that, to survive, and hopefully in the longer term to prosper, York must devise ways in which the usurping House of Lancaster could be replaced in the seat of power by the legitimate heir to the throne, namely himself.

He had said nothing of this to his family, nor to his nephew Richard Neville when he visited Ireland prior to the victorious return of the three Earls from Calais. Thus Warwick was totally taken by surprise when the Duke of York, having led a great procession of Lords and Bishops into the King's Council Chamber, laid his hand on the vacant throne, symbolically taking possession of this ultimate token of Kingship, and then turned to face the assembly, clearly awaiting their approving applause.

None came, instead Canterbury asked the Duke if he wished to attend on the King, to which York replied that he knew of no man in the Kingdom who should not come to him rather than he go to them. He then moved through into the King's private apartments, having his men break door-locks where necessary and stayed there some while inspecting the rooms and their appointments with a proprietorial air. As York left the Palace, he was confronted by Warwick, who saw his own plans to run the Kingdom, through the medium of the captive Henry, crash in ruins before this blossoming of his uncle's ambition and a blazing row ensued.

However, York would not be dissuaded from his purpose and insisted on presenting a lengthy justification of his claim to the crown to the assembled Parliament. His line descended directly from Lionel of Clarence, second surviving son of Edward III, while the Lancastrian claim was based on descent from John of Gaunt, third son of King Edward and the current, sickly representative of the line owed his Royal state initially to the usurpation by his grandfather, Henry Bolingbroke, of Richard II's throne.

Although there could be no denial of the justice of York's claim, the Lords and Commons noted that the House of Lancaster had ruled the land for 60 years and the great Paladin-king, Henry of Monmouth, had made England a respected power in the world. In the end, therefore, it was agreed and enacted through the Act of Accord that Henry should rule for his lifetime, with York acting as his chief minister and his ultimate successor; and this text, cancelling his own son's right to succeed him, the weak King duly signed into Law.

This charade of peaceful settlement through compromise satisfied King Henry and, probably, the Duke of York. The Earl of Warwick, however, knew that the dispossessed heir-apparent's mother, Margaret of Anjou, would never consent to her son's rights being dismissed so peremptorily and he devoted his time to planning measures against the troubles he knew would come - and quickly.

Following the defeat at Northampton, Queen Margaret with her son had made her way into Wales and eventually reached the safe haven of Jasper Tudor's castle at Pembroke. From here she made contact with Somerset, still in Guisnes trying to make good his now-redundant appointment to be Captain of Calais, telling him to return to his west country estates, to raise armed levies and to move these northwards as quickly as might be. Margaret likewise sent messengers to her friends in the northwest, Lords Clifford and Neville, and to Harry Percy at Alnwick, asking them to raise and arm men, and prepare to join her shortly in Yorkshire, where they would rendezvous with Somerset, and John Courtenay, Earl of Devon, and all their force.

Spurred by the news of York's return and of his claim to the succession, the Lords of Lancaster worked mightily through the last months of 1460 to raise a great army. Lord John Neville, brother to the Earl of Westmorland, secured a commission from the Duke to raise men in the border country, under the pretext that these would be available to support the Yorkist cause. Armed with this official authorisation, Neville raised 8,000 hard-bitten fighting men, mainly Scottish reivers, in record time on promises of the rich loot to be gathered from the Border and, mayhap, all the way south to London. This horde of ravagers joined with Clifford's Cumbrians and Percy's Northumbrians and the northern men met with the Queen, Somerset and Devon as planned, north of the Humber at November's end.

The great, and growing, Lancastrian army moved slowly westwards towards the Great North Road, down which they expected to march to London, and, being short of money and supplies, its leaders gave full licence to their men to live off the country around them, virtually all of which was owned by the Duke of York and Richard Neville, Earl of Salisbury. By the 10th of December, the two leaders of the Yorkist faction were headed north from London with a well-armed and mounted force of 2,500 men, empowered by Royal Commission to restore order in Yorkshire and the northern counties. In bitter Winter weather, the Yorkists reached Sandal, the Duke's great castle just south of Wakefield on December 21st and rested there to celebrate the Feast of the Nativity.

With the castle's garrison, the total force lodged in Sandal exceeded 3,000 and it soon became necessary to send out foraging parties to replenish their supplies and to put out scouts to locate the raiding Lancastrians, whose exact whereabouts and numbers were unknown to York and Salisbury. On December 29th, the Yorkist reconnaissance brushed against Lancastrian pickets at Pontefract, where the bulk of the Queen's army was billeted, and, under questioning, prisoners revealed the presence of York and Salisbury at Sandal and the comparative weakness of the force with them.

With Somerset sick in bed, Margaret conferred with Clifford - the fiercest of her generals - and they agreed to move the 12 miles west towards Sandal early the following morning with the force they had with them, which hugely outnumbered the Yorkist army. Late in the afternoon of December 30th, 1460 the army of Lancaster was arrayed in three divisions below Sandal's walls, challenging their enemies to come down and fight. Whether discretion would have proved the better part of valour under all the circumstances will never be known, since Margaret's arrival coincided with the expected return of York's foragers and, unless the leaders were prepared to sacrifice men and supplies, there was no option other than to attack in the hope of breaking through to safety.

Quickly, the men of York armed themselves and mounted in the courtyard and Baileys, the gates were thrown back, the portcullis raised and Richard Plantagenet, with his second son, Edmund, Earl of Rutland, and Richard

WAKEFIELD. DECEMBER 30th 1460.

Sandal Magna Church.

Wakefield

ROOS

YORK

WILTSHIRE

MARGARET & CLIFFORD.

Calder

N

Neville, Earl of Salisbury, likewise with his second son, Sir Thomas, emerged from the castle, formed their line and charged down on the jeering Lancastrians.

The centre of the three divisions, where the banners of Queen Margaret rose alongside the gold and blue 'checkies' of Clifford, was the main target of the Yorkist charge and the initial force of their clash drove the Lancastrian line backwards towards the River Calder immediately in their rear, giving momentary hope of an unlikely victory to the roaring cavalry of Neville and Plantagenet. But, Clifford and his captains rallied their line and the divisions to left and right led by Lord Roos, standing in for his step-brother, Somerset, and James Butler, Earl of Wiltshire. closed in on the Yorkist flanks and their charge was enveloped in the suffocating hordes of the Queen's army. The end was inevitable, given Lancaster's crushing superiority in numbers and, although some gallant riders broke through and escaped across the bridge to Wakefield town, near 3,000 went down to defeat and death in the battle and the pursuit.

Among the dead were Richard, Duke of York, his son, Rutland, and Sir Thomas Neville. Richard Neville, Earl of Salisbury, survived battle and aftermath, being taken for ransom and lodged in Pontefract Castle. Unhappily, his remission was short-lived, and the following morning he was hauled from his cell, allegedly "by common people which loved him not", and lynched in the castle courtyard. Traditionally, Rutland was murdered on Wakefield bridge as he tried to make good his escape, by "Bloody Clifford", who taunted the captive York with his son's pitiful end, before similarly ending the Duke's life. Whatever the truth of the stories, the heads of the three were displayed on the Micklegate Bar at York and Richard Planatgenet's bloody brow was encircled by a mock crown of paper and straw, visible testimony of Queen Margaret's views on the Act of Accord.

With the chief of her enemies disposed of, the Queen drew her army together and commenced a slow advance south towards London, where waited the sole - and most hated - survivor of the trio who had disinherited her son, Richard Neville, Earl of Warwick. From the reports which she had no doubt would have flown south from Sandal, Warwick would now know the price for treason against the Queen's majesty and Margaret, Clifford and Somerset looked forward to presenting his reckoning in short course.

CHAPTER TEN

St Albans Revisited.

Following their victory at Wakefield and the deaths of the Yorkist leaders, the Lancastrians found recruiting easy across northern England, and still more Scottish moss troopers flocked south to join the Queen's force. By mid-January an unwieldy, ill-disciplined mass numbering close on 40,000 set off south for London and pillaged and burned a track 30 miles wide from Wakefield to Luton, which they reached on February 14th. Here they halted to regroup and gather much-needed supplies from the surrounding country. Scouts sent to the south returned with news that Richard Neville had disposed a large army in and around St Albans and was barring their way to London.

The Earl of Warwick had received the bitter news from Wakefield around January 5th and had immediately left his own estates, where he had been celebrating Christmastide with his family, and returned to the capital. Here he summoned the supporters of York from the southern and eastern counties and his own people from the Midlands, and sent word to Edward of March, who was away recruiting men in the Welsh Marches around Ludlow and Leominster, to complete his work and join Warwick's main force as quickly as possible. Then, leading an army of some 20,000 men he moved forward to St Albans, the traditional northern gateway to London, and on February 12th made ready to receive the oncoming Lancastrian masses.

Richard Neville, Earl of Warwick and now of Salisbury, was the great planner of his party and of his time. Not for him the uncontrolled cut and thrust of bloody close-quarters combat, the rising dust, the metallic clangour, the roaring battle-cries and the screams of the dying; rather would he pre-plan an engagement in intricate detail, anticipate his enemies' strokes and prepare his parry and counter-thrust, plan and scheme and out-think his adversary before ever a blow had been struck. And, when the action was joined, Neville would stand in the background, watching the working-out of his immaculate masterpiece, making minor adjustments here and there as the fighting developed, the puppet-master pulling the strings, forcing the enemy into mistakes, errors of judgement, catastrophe. This was how he would fight for a second time at St Albans - this was how he would bring the House of York to the brink of final disaster.

Warwick based his plans on fighting a defensive battle aimed at stopping the Lancastrians in their tracks at St Albans and driving them away from London. He knew the enemy was approaching from the north and of the two main approach roads they could take to his chosen battle site, he assumed the more likely was the western route from Luton/Harpenden. His supposition may have been influenced by the existence of an old Celtic earthwork, Beech Bottom, which crossed this road, and gave any defending force a strong rampart against their attackers. Here he based his main division under the immediate command of his brother, John, created Lord Montagu on the earls' return from Calais, and he set the men to strengthening their position with novel secret weapons, which Warwick felt would cause consternation among the ranks of Lancaster when they advanced to the attack.

The new war materials included wide mesh cord netting to spread over the ground with upright spikes knotted-in at every second loop. Archers and hand-gunners had shields with loopholes through which they could shoot and then close-up while they reloaded. The backs of the shields were studded with spikes to form an unpleasant obstacle to the further advance of attacking troops when thrown down before them, and a spiked lattice similar to the netting in purpose, but moveable, was also designed to harm oncoming foes, as were the caltrops - four-pointed devices which could be scattered before cavalry with one spike always upwards. And for the gunners, themselves somewhat of a novelty, long arrows with 'mighty heads of iron' and 'wildfire' were provided.

Warwick's second position blocking the east side approach from Harpenden he located at the village of Sandridge some three miles north of St Albans, and equipped his division there equally with his new defensive weapons. This he decided would be his own position, commanding the centre and the effective reserve and able to move his men to either flank as the impending action developed. As a 'trip-wire' and flank guard, he sent a smaller division composed mainly of East Anglians under John Mowbray, Duke of Norfolk, further along the road to the appropriately named 'No Mans Land' and located a strong mobile reserve of Yorkshire archers in the town square at St Albans, where they could also provide an anchor for his left flank. His preparations completed by the morning of February 16th, he settled to await developments and sent scouts to the north to check on the approach of Margaret's army, including a strong group of 200 lances which he ordered up Watling Street to Dunstable, from where they could view the advance of Lancaster to their east and report back on the enemy's progress as necessary.

Richard Neville had thus split his (smaller) army into four sections, each separated from the others by a mile or more, thus committing the cardinal error of dividing his force in the face of the enemy and, to crown this, his efforts to check closely on the approach of his adversaries were to draw their attack in such a way that Warwick's strong defensive positions were all facing in entirely the wrong direction. Not a promising start for a would-be master tactician.

The ponderously advancing Queen's army, constantly slowed and halted by the need to find supplies for the vast assembly of men and animals on their 200 mile trail from Yorkshire, had called in its foragers on the news of Warwick's presence. By late afternoon of February 16th the Lancastrians were preparing to advance south towards St Albans, when news came from their scouts that a strong body of horse had been seen at Dunstable, possibly the advance guard of Warwick's army moving against their right flank. Eager for what she intended to be a final meeting with Richard Neville, Margaret urged her army to move with all speed to Dunstable and a large force of cavalry sent as advance guard succeeded in capturing or killing the Yorkist outpost.

Under questioning, the captives made clear that Warwick was standing on the defensive in and around St Albans and, most likely, with an inferior force, numerically, to their own. Although darkness was now fast approaching, Margaret's eagerness to come to blows with her enemies was not to be denied and under her furious urging, her captains, Somerset, Clifford, Lord John Neville, and Andrew Trollope, whose fortune had risen high since his desertion of Warwick at Ludford Bridge, led the whole army forward on a 12 mile night-march down Watling Street heading directly for St Albans. Here they arrived just as morning lightened the Winter skies, having - by pure chance - by-passed all Warwick's carefully prepared defences, and their advance guard flung themselves on the newly-rising garrison of archers in the town square.

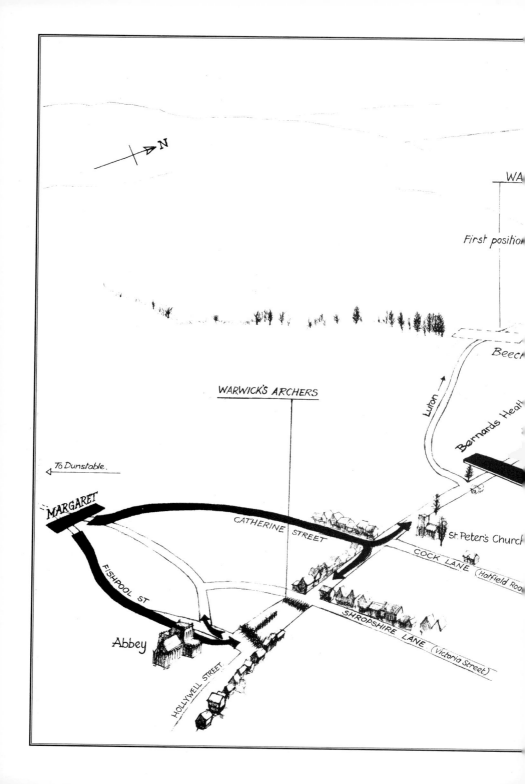

N

WA

First positio

Beec

Luton

Bernards Heat

WARWICK'S ARCHERS

To Dunstable.

MARGARET

CATHERINE STREET

St. Peter's Church

COCK LANE (Hatfield Roa

FISHPOOL ST

SHROPSHIRE LANE (Victoria Street)

Abbey

HOLLYWELL STREET

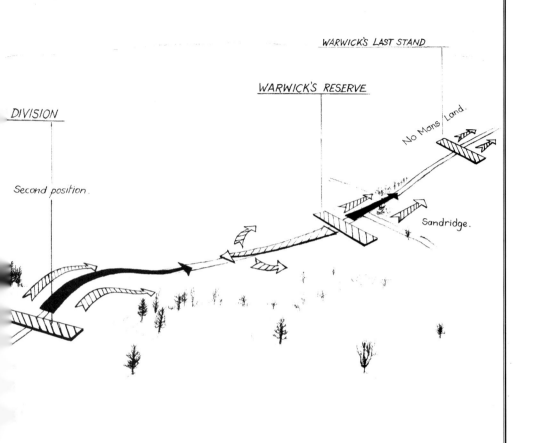

WARWICK'S LAST STAND

WARWICK'S RESERVE

DIVISION

Second position.

No Mans Land.

Sandridge.

Second St. ALBANS.
February 17th 1461.

Although taken by surprise, the bowmen were experienced men of war and quickly formed lines and loosed volley after volley on their attackers, who were driven back up their original line of attack down Fishpool Street by the Abbey. However, hardly had the Yorkshiremen time for mutual congratulation on repelling the incursion, when more foes charged them in the rear, having found an alternative approach via Catherine Street. The archers were now under attack from both sides and, arrows exhausted, were fighting hand-to-hand with opponents who out-matched them in numbers and liked nothing better than   a close-quarters street-brawl fight. The end was inevitable, but the archers died hard and the clamour of their last fight aroused the sleeping Earl of Warwick to consciousness of his danger and the wreck of all his carefully laid plans. Arming himself as he rode, he spurred away from the first onslaught towards his main division at Beech Bottom.

Here his men were ending their morning meal and looking back down the road behind them wondering at the growing roar of battle from the town. When Warwick arrived he ordered his brother John to take his men out of their established position and to face about, form line and take with them as much of their new defensive paraphernalia as they could quickly move. Fortunately for Montagu, the Yorkshiremen's plucky fight to the death gave them time to relocate their position and the initial reluctance of the victorious Lancastrians to engage this new line of foes, rather than commence their customary looting, enabled his men to move many of Warwick's ground obstacles into the path of the finally-approaching Lancastrian horde.

This time, the attackers had no element of surprise to aid them and the Yorkist line gave a very good account of itself, holding the enemy's assaults and repeatedly throwing them back. Montagu knew that Warwick, having watched them starting their move into the new position, had ridden on to Sandridge to bring up the reserve division stationed there and he encouraged his men with shouts that strong reinforcements were coming, which would enable them to turn the tables on the Lancastrians and extract payment for the deaths of their comrades. Unhappily for this scenario, Richard Neville was finding it difficult, to say the least, to persuade the Sandridge men to leave their position and move up the hill towards the roar of battle which grew ever louder beyond the crest of the ridge behind them.

By mid-afternoon, however, the Sandridge men agreed to move up to the support of their embattled line and started up the rise, while Warwick spurred away yet again to bring up the last reinforcing element of his army from No

Mans Land. As he did so, the line of his main division, denied the awaited support for so long, folded and broke and a fleeing rabble came over the brow of the hill above the advancing third division and crashed into it, followed immediately by chasing, cursing, killing Lancastrian troops.

The effect was devastating. Warwick's army was shattered and the defeated Earl could do no more than flog his tired horse into another gallop to join Norfolk and the last of his men at No Mans Land. As night fell over the stricken field of Second St Albans, leaving his brother Montagu and many others captive to the victorious, uproariously-celebrating Lancastrians, Warwick used the sheltering dark to lead the remnant of his army away to the west, where he hoped to join with Edward of March's force and plan again for another and better day.

Garter Stall Plate of John Neville, Marquis Montagu.

(St George's Chapel, Windsor)

Edward IV

(Society of Artiquaries of London)

CHAPTER ELEVEN

This Glorious Sonne of York.

Warwick found the young Edward - he had not yet celebrated his twentieth birthday - and his men moving south from Burford in Oxfordshire, and the two armies, after a short rest, made directly and speedily for London. Edward's force was in much better shape, physically and morale-wise than Neville's, since they came fresh from an astonishing victory on February 2nd over a larger and better-equipped army of Welshmen, led by Jasper Tudor, Earl of Pembroke.

The Earl of March had met Tudor at Mortimer's Cross, near Leominster, as the Welshman moved towards Worcester, hoping to cut Edward's route to London. There, aided by William Hastings, a gentleman of Warwickshire who had brought a strong, well-armed body of men to join his force, and by the appearance of a parhelion - a seeming-triple sun - over the field, which the quick-thinking Edward had proclaimed as a sign of heavenly favour, he had given the enemy a sound drubbing and better-equipped his army from the arms of the fallen.

The news of this success put new heart into Richard Neville and his men, and as the combined force closed on London, the Earl of Warwick was seeing his young cousin in an entirely new perspective. This strapping young man - he was nearly six and a half feet tall - was clearly a fighting-man of unusual mettle. Warwick had seen him break into the Lancastrian position at Northampton, alongside the experienced Fauconberg, and now, in a sole command, he had whipped a more-experienced, stronger opponent, shown the foresight to re-equip his army from the arms and armour of the defeated foe, and demonstrated a strong degree of ruthlessness by publicly beheading the ancient Owen Tudor, father of Jasper and second husband to the widow of Henry V, in the market square of Haverfordwest.

Furthermore, Edward was a handsome, as well as imposing, figure - Warwick recalled he had been called the Rose of Rouen in his recent youth - and would make a marvellous instrument through which Richard Neville might control the Yorkist faction and the Kingdom. As soon as the immediate negotiations with the City Fathers had been accomplished, Warwick decided he would seize this new, heaven-sent opportunity to revive the fortunes of the Yorkists, whom he now led, and - equally important - those of the House of Neville of Middleham, of which he had become titular head. He, Earl of Warwick and Salisbury, now the most powerful Peer in England, would make a new King.

On the 4th of March, 1461, Edward rode in state to Westminster Abbey and before the high altar declared his title to the crown and sat on the throne, carrying the sceptre of the Confessor in his hand, to receive the fealty of his subjects. That done, he retired to the Tower where he made his lodgings, and while heralds proclaimed in every street that Edward, fourth of that name, was by the advice of the Lords Spiritual, Temporal, and the election of the Commons, crowned ruler of France and England, and Lord of Ireland, the victor of Mortimer's Cross sat with Richard and William Neville, and John Mowbray to plan their next meeting with the brawling mass of rogues who made up the undefeated army of Margaret of Anjou.

The Queen's forces had made their normally slow progress towards London after their victory. Queen Margaret, having regained her husband, who was found sitting happily under an oak tree near No Mans Land, chatting with his friendly custodians (who were promptly beheaded, despite Henry's protests, on his wife's orders) had tried to drive the men on to the real prize, but the overwhelming size of her force, and its consequent indiscipline, had prevented this.

When they finally reached the walls, a deputation was sent, on the advice of John Morton, clergyman, lawyer, clerk to the King's Council and valued adviser to Her Majesty, to demand that the King and Queen should be admitted to their capital. The City Fathers, confident now in the strength of their defences, had no hesitation in refusing this request, and, after some blustering, the Lancastrian army turned its steps northwards again, needing fresh and more-friendly country to support its numbers. Immediately behind them, Warwick spurred for his Midlands estates and Norfolk for East Anglia, while Fauconberg again scoured Kent for willing bowmen and infantry. The new King would soon have a new army to lead and a heavy reckoning would be presented to the Lords of Lancaster.

On March 11th, William Neville, Lord Fauconberg, swung boldly through London's gate leading the advance guard of York's new army, mainly archers and light infantry from Kent and the Welsh Marches. The next day, King Edward led the balance of his forces out of his capital and followed the line of Fauconberg's march, linking en route with Warwick and Norfolk. By the 25th of the month, a great army was assembled at Pontefract and, already, scouts were pushing forward from ancient Pomfret castle, feeling outwards, searching, for the army of Margaret of Anjou.

When no contacts were made south of the River Aire, Warwick went forward at dawn on Saturday, March 28th with a troop of cavalry to reconnoitre and capture the crossing at Ferrybridge. Unhappily for him, the location of the Yorkist army had been known to the Queen and Somerset for some days, and Lord Clifford, who had already secured the crossing and broken the bridge, now lay in wait for unwary Yorkists with a strong force of mounted archers. The arrow volleys from Clifford's ambush killed or dismounted many of Warwick's men and the Earl was himself slightly wounded in the leg.

Panicking in the uproar and confusion so reminiscent of the savage brawl at St Albans, Richard Neville turned his plunging horse around and fled the two miles back down the road to where Edward waited with the main force. The young King was not impressed with the new disaster which had befallen his cousin and immediately sent Fauconberg and his mounted archers forward to probe the flanks of Clifford's position for an alternative way across. This, William Neville located four miles upstream at Castleford and, sending word to Edward of his intention, the old warrior crossed the Aire and advanced towards the right flank of Clifford's force holding Ferrybridge.

Edward wasted no time in pressing forward to the river, and Clifford soon finding himself outnumbered and assailed from front and flank, decided discretion was the better part on this occasion. He ordered his men to mount up and fall back on their main force, which Somerset had drawn up on a low ridge just south of a tiny Yorkshire community, which would give its name to the greatest battle ever fought on English soil. It was the village of Towton. Unhappily for John Clifford - and for the fortunes of Lancaster - he delayed his order to retire a fraction too long and, during the flight to safety, somewhere up the narrow road through Dintingdale, Clifford took an arrow through the neck and died shortly after, taking no part in the monumental struggle which was to follow.

Edward reached another ridge to the south of Towton in the late afternoon and saw the great army of Lancaster drawn up across a facing rise in the ground, its flanks protected by woods and ravines, a position strong enough to daunt the bravest. The young King marshalled his own forces in a line directly opposite the foe and, like the Lancastrians, found the chosen battle-ground was too narrow for the number of men in his army. He, therefore, arrayed them in depth across and behind the available frontage and since darkness was now falling, and Norfolk's strong division had not yet come up with the main army, he settled down to wait for morning. Because of the proximity of the enemy, the men had to rest in their lines, wearing their mail or stiff leather jacks, and on a bitterly cold night, few got much sleep. With the morning light, the wind blowing from behind the Yorkist lines strengthened and snow flurries gusted into the faces of the waiting men of Lancaster.

William, Lord Fauconberg, met with his two nephews in a Council of War and they agreed that, with their smaller force - Norfolk had still not rejoined, being delayed by illness - and the lack of space for manoeuvre, it would be best to await an attack from the enemy. Further, since the Lancastrians apparently also preferred to await an attack, Fauconberg would employ a trick he had learned in the French wars to prick them into action. Edward agreed with this and himself took the central command in the front of the Yorkist position; Richard Neville he stationed in the rear of the army to perform his, now customary, role in control of the reserve.

About ten of the clock, Fauconberg directed his archers to filter through the front lines of men-at-arms and advance towards the enemy. When they were within bowshot, trumpets sounded, the advancing lines halted and suddenly showers of arrows and crossbow bolts mingled with the snow which a howling, gale-force wind was blizzarding into the faces of the Lancastrians. The volleys released, the archers - as they had been instructed - immediately retired a short way and the vigorous response from Lancaster's bowmen into the gale fell well short of their target. As their fire diminished, the spent shafts were recovered and returned with interest by Fauconberg's men and the army of Lancaster, now lacking ammunition to continue the action at long range and suffering increasing casualties from the seemingly unending fire of the Yorkists, moved forward off their ridge, crossed the intervening dip, and closed with the waiting foemen.

The battle now became an awful slogging match with no quarter asked or

TOWTON. March 29th 1461. First Phase: Morning.

TOWTON. March 29th 1461.   Second Phase: Afternoon.

N

Tadcaster.

Towton.

To Ferrybridge →

NORFOLK

SOMERSET

EDWARD

WARWICK

To Saxton →

Renshaw Wood.

Bloody Meadow

River Cock.

Castle Hill Wood.

given and the killing continued hour after hour towards the late afternoon. Many times the bodies of the slain would pile up and form barriers of corpses between the battling lines, only to be flung aside and trampled as the two sides continued their terrible grappling match to the death. Eventually, the greater numbers of Lancaster took their toll of Edward's men, and the wings of his lines were pressing back and back, when, as the evening dusk fell, relief came as Norfolk and his fresh division at last arrived and immediately thrust forward down the right flank of Edward's army.

This infusion of fresh troops was too much for the tiring Lancastrians, who were pressed back and across the bloody, frozen field until they broke and ran. The majority fled down the frozen slopes of the ravine through which flowed the Cock Beck, now in full spate with the heavy rain and snow-water, and tired and wounded men died, drowned in the murky freezing torrent, until sufficient had perished to form human bridges across which their erstwhile comrades could prolong their own flight.

The surviving leaders, the Duke of Somerset among them, who had kept their chargers handy behind the fighting, made good their escape to York and thence north towards the succour of the Scottish Border country, accompanied by Queen Margaret and her son, and the hapless Henry VI, once more a King without crown or throne, or even a safe place to lay his weary, confused head.

On the next morning - the day after Palm Sunday, 1461 - while the victorious army dug grave pits in which to inter their own and the much more plentiful Lancastrian dead, King Edward wrote dutifully to his mother to tell her of his great victory, which must assure the throne to York, and said that the number of the slain was 28,000. Among them were Courtenay, Earl of Devon, Lord Clifford, the killer of Edward's father and brother after Wakefield, (though his body was not found on the field) Lord Dacre, half-Clifford through his mother, along with - still better news for the Nevilles - Henry Percy, Earl of Northumberland and Lord John Neville, brother of the Earl of Westmorland. To complete their familial triumph, Warwick's brother, Lord Montagu, captured at Second St Albans, was found in York, safe and well and ready to resume service against Lancaster.

His opportunity to strike back at his former captors would not wait long. Edward, whose first task had been to order the removal of the heads of his father and brother and of Richard Neville, Earl of Salisbury from Micklegate Bar, then kept Easter at York and in Warwick's Keep at Middleham. He was briefly in Durham, where Laurence Booth submitted to his royal authority and was made King's Confessor for his change of coat, and went on to Newcastle where the fugitive Earl of Wiltshire, the handsomest Peer in the Realm, who had fled Towton as quickly as First St Albans, was brought before him and was promptly beheaded.

Some three weeks after Towton, the young King led his triumphant army south to London to re-celebrate his victory in the midst of his most adoring citizens, while Richard and John Neville stayed and took stock of their force at Middleham. There would be much work for them there and thereabouts, when the Scottish avengers, spurred on by Margaret and backed by French gold, had shaken off the shock of defeat and returned to their Border raiding.

Barnard Castle, Durham.
From an Engraving by W. Byrne.

(Geoffrey Wheeler)

72

CHAPTER TWELVE

Border Wars and Diplomacy

𝕴t took only two months for the resilient Scots reivers to recover their traditional esprit and 6,000 of them came boiling over the Border aiming for Carlisle, which Queen Margaret had given them licence to sack. Warwick had good notice of their coming through his Border-watchers and John Neville surprised them in the field as they set out their siege-lines round the town's walls and sent them packing north again, bloodied and empty-handed.

This early raid set the pattern for much of the next three years, when John Neville would be constantly employed in driving raiding parties led by Scots or Lancastrian exiles away from their intended targets and, where possible, relieving them of any booty they might have gathered during their shortened forays into northern England. Immediately, with Warwick, he commenced an ongoing campaign against Lancastrian supporters holding out in northern castles, and here Warwick's preference for the methodical, planned approach to warfare stood the Nevilles in good stead. King Edward had made his kinsman Warden of both Western and Eastern Marches and using all the authority conveyed by these titles, Richard Neville and his brother moved east and north across the land and by October-end, the Percies' strongholds of Alnwick and Dunstanburgh had surrendered to their all-conquering Yorkist besiegers.

Warwick, feeling that the north country was reasonably peaceful again, answered Edward's summons to a Parliament in November and occupied himself in London and on his own estates for some months. Early in 1462, however, following an abortive rising by an old Lancastrian, the Earl of Oxford, which was quickly and ruthlessly quelled, Richard Neville had to return north to negotiate with Mary of Guelders, Queen Dowager of the Scots, whom he hoped could influence the Council of Regency to call off the constant border attacks. In this he was unsuccessful, but his visit may have been instrumental in Queen Mary making a loan to Margaret of Anjou to finance her move to France, where she hoped to sue successfully for aid at the court of the new King, Louis XI.

Failing in his quest for peace, Warwick 'let slip the dogs of war' and John Neville, aided by the newly ennobled Lords William Hastings and Robert Ogle, raided deep into Scottish territory to such effect that their opponents were glad to agree a Summer truce. With the Scots at least temporarily quiet, the Nevilles returned again to siege work against the Northumbrian castles still loyal to Lancaster and their forces were thus occupied when Margaret with her old friend, Piers de Brezé, the butcher of Sandwich, and King Henry, landed at Bamburgh Castle towards the end of October.

The mixed French and Scottish force moved into Dunstanburgh and Alnwick and began to march southwards, hoping to draw support from the local population. This was not forthcoming in significant strength and learning that the Nevilles were moving towards them and only awaiting the arrival of Edward with substantial reinforcements before attacking, Margaret and de Brezé garrisoned the three castles strongly under the overall command of Somerset, and took ship for Scotland, promising to return with a new army.

With no opposing army in the field, Edward left it to Warwick to concentrate his undoubted organisational talents on laying siege again to Alnwick, Bamburgh and Dunstanburgh. He gave command of the first leaguer to his uncle, Lord Fauconberg, now Earl of Kent; Bamburgh was besieged by his brother John and Lord Ogle; Dunstanburgh by John Tiptoft, Earl of Worcester. Warwick commanded the strong reserve force based at Warkworth Castle, and from there, constantly checked the progress of the three operations and the security of their central supply base at Newcastle, from where Norfolk was responsible for supplying the besiegers.

Hungry, worn down by the constant pressure exerted by Richard Neville and his commanders, and finally despairing of relief from Scotland, Somerset and the garrisons at Bamburgh and Dunstanburgh surrendered in the two days following Christmas, 1462. The men and officers were disarmed and allowed to depart, Somerset was sent to Edward for judgement and exerting his Beaufort charm to the uttermost, succeeded in becoming a close friend and boon companion to the King for much of the following year. Meantime, Warwick had personally taken over supervision of his final operation, against Alnwick, and was pressing his siege when, on January 5th, the Earl of Angus and Piers de Brezé appeared with a relieving army of several thousand men. Warwick, with events at Ferrybridge - and Second St Albans - burned deeply into his mind, immediately called all his men to mount and led them, not towards but away from, the Scots' force.

The relieved garrison opened their gates and joyfully welcomed their deliverers, urging pursuit of the fast-disappearing Englishmen, but Angus, a canny Border Scot, suspected a trap and refused to be tricked into ambush by the wily Warwick. Instead, he retraced his steps back over the Border, and the erstwhile garrison went with him, leaving Alnwick an easy capture for the returning Neville forces the following day.

By Spring, the north was quietened sufficiently for Richard Neville to travel south again to attend Parliament and to apply his diplomatic skills in discussions with Ambassadors from Louis of France and Philip of Burgundy. At the end of May, however, news came from Montagu that Piers de Brezé had crossed the Border again with a strong force of Scots, French, and English exiles and the three main castles had immediately surrendered to his summons on behalf of Lancaster. Once more, Warwick rode northwards taking men-at-arms with him to join forces with his brother.

And yet again, Warwick's skilled organisation combined with Montagu's fierceness in battle to overwhelm the Lancastrian army and the Nevilles continued to pursue their beaten foes well into the Lowlands of Scotland, where they caused such havoc as to force the Scots to sue for a further truce. Edward came north to sign the document on December 9th and, meantime, Margaret of Anjou feeling her cause was lost had left Scotland for France taking her son with her. King Henry was under siege in impregnable Bamburgh Castle and the remaining Lancastrian troops were similarly penned in Dunstanburgh and Alnwick.

Again, the north was secure and again Warwick made his way to London in the Spring of 1464 for further talks with the French Ambassador. And, yet again, the smouldering embers of Lancaster blazed up across Northumberland, this time at the instigation of Henry Beaufort, Duke of Somerset, erstwhile bosom friend of King Edward, who had reverted to his Lancastrian roots and joined King Henry at Bamburgh. From here he raided constantly with support from Lord Roos, the veteran of Wakefield, Sir Ralph Percy, Lord Hungerford, and the rest of the die-hard Lancastrians still disputing the Yorkist rule along the Border.

Montagu had been made Warden of the East March in the previous Summer, to ease Warwick's apparent burden and in recognition of his own fighting qualities. He was therefore able to raise levies in his own right, after sending word of events to the King and his brother, and was soon in action against the rebels. While en route to escort a party of Scottish nobles towards York, where they were due to meet commissioners appointed by Edward, Montagu learned his party was to be ambushed by a strong force led by Sir Humphrey Neville, son to Lord John who had died at Towton, and Sir Ralph Percy whose older brother, the then Earl of Northumberland, had died in the same fight.

With prior intelligence of the impending attack, Montagu made for Newcastle where he gathered his garrison, and marched out against his would-be assailants. Realising they had missed their chance, the Lancastrians were making the best of their way to safety when Montagu caught them at Hedgley Moor, scattering and killing them. Ralph Percy would not see Alnwick again, but Humphrey Neville escaped to rebel and be reconciled time and again, before Edward finally decided enough was enough and had him executed in 1469.

The triumphant Montagu returned to his original course and took the Scots safely on to York, then returning to his headquarters at Newcastle to await the arrival of the King and Warwick. Hardly had he arrived, when news came that Somerset and King Henry with a substantial force were 15 miles to the west of the town and had made camp there, as though inviting battle. John Neville needed no second invitation and waiting no longer for reinforcement, marched out to meet the treacherous Beaufort, whose life King Edward had already ordained was forfeit on capture. Paralleling the ancient defences of the land built by the Roman Emperor Hadrian against the Scots, John, Lord Montagu led his eager cavalry forward towards the small, insignificant town of Hexham.

John Neville's scouts soon located the enemy on a patch of flat ground, roughly half a mile square, called Hexham Levels which lay to the southeast of the town. Alerted by his own reconnaissance, Somerset had hastily drawn up his forces in two divisions whose flanks and rear were protected by a small, steeply-banked stream, but whose position would be perilous in the extreme were they to be caught between the ravine and a strong attack. This is exactly the fate that befell Henry Beaufort, since Montagu arriving at the head of a slope down towards the Levels immediately saw the inherent weakness of Somerset's formation and, without more ado, swung his men

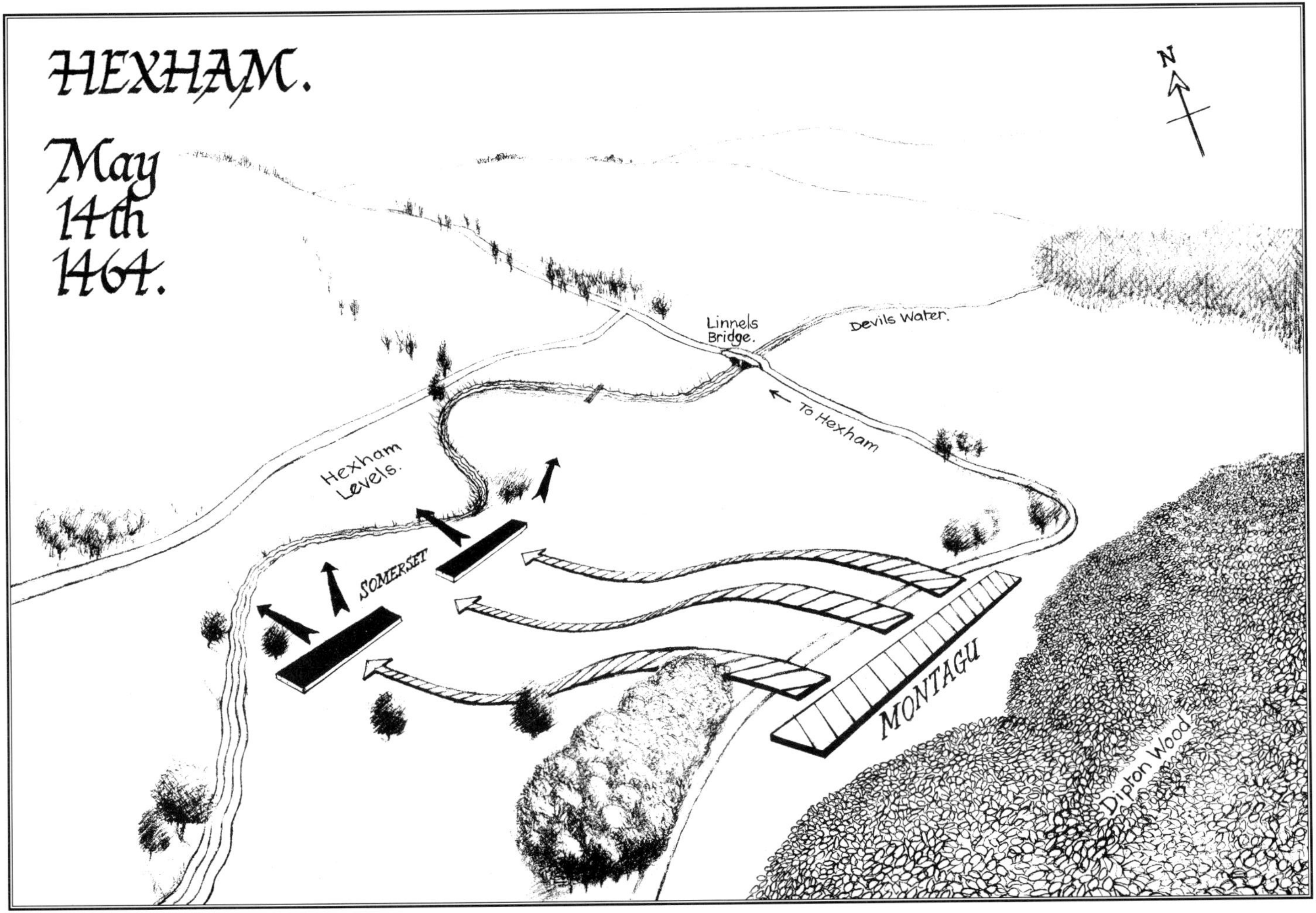
HEXHAM.
May
14th
1464.
N
Linnels Bridge.
Devils Water.
To Hexham
Hexham Levels.
SOMERSET
MONTAGU
Dipton Wood

from column into line, and charged down on the nervous Lancastrians.

The effect was catastrophic, the force of the Yorkists' charge hit the standing lines of Somerset's men and drove them backwards into and down the waiting ravine. The action was over in minutes, the troops of Lancaster saved themselves if they could, though most died before they were able to make good their escape. The hapless King Henry who had located himself strategically towards the left of the line and well to the rear, was able to skirt round the Yorkists' right flank and, with a few retainers, made his way southwest into Lancashire and wandered there and in Scotland for a time, before being betrayed, captured and sent to the Tower for safe lodging. Less fortunate, Lord Roos was found amongst the dead and Somerset, wounded and captured on the field, was taken to Hexham and there beheaded in the market square.

When King Edward arrived in York two weeks later, he found the work had already been done for him and was mightily pleased with the solutions Montagu had found to the recent troubles. He immediately created him Earl of Northumberland with all the estates pertaining to the title, which had formerly been held by the Nevilles' chief rivals in the north, the Percies. Now the Nevilles ruled a great swathe of territory across the whole of northern England and with Warwick's lands in the Midlands, the southern counties and into Wales they were the greatest Peers and the mightiest force in the land.

This point was not lost on the King, who, while on his way north to join with the Nevilles, had taken a long step towards establishing a counter-power in the land. Without Warwick's knowledge, Edward had taken a wife.

CHAPTER THIRTEEN

"And when the Earl of Warwick came home and
heard hereof, then was he greatly displeased..."
(Warkworth Chronicle)

His business in north Yorkshire done, the King turned south again and occupied himself and his troops with a siege of Skipton Castle which, faithful to its Clifford Heritage, had taken advantage of the recent stirring to come out for Lancaster. Warwick and Montagu moved northwards to retake the Northumbrian castles and on June 23rd appeared before Alnwick, which surrendered immediately to its new Earl, on promise of the garrison's lives. Dunstanburgh and Norham quickly followed suit and only the virtually impregnable Bamburgh was left holding out for Lancaster. This was not surprising since the commanders were Sir Ralph Grey, a former retainer of the Middleham Nevilles who had betrayed Alnwick to Lancaster the year before, and Sir Humphrey Neville whose ambush had so nearly accounted for Montagu only weeks before. Neither could expect quarter at the hands of John and Richard Neville.

The Earl of Warwick, ever-interested in new developments, may have rejoiced at the intransigence of Sir Ralph and Sir Humphrey since it gave him an opportunity to use the great siege guns the King had brought north for just such an eventuality. And 'Newcastle' and 'London', the greatest guns, with 'Dijon', 'Edward' and 'Richard' - the last, perhaps, named for the Earl himself - shot their missiles continuously against and over the castle's walls until "Presently the wall was breached, and my Lord of Warwick, with his men-at-arms and archers, won the castle by assault..." Humphrey Neville, ever-elusive, made his escape; Sir Ralph Grey, less fortunate, was taken and sent to Doncaster before the King.

There, John Tiptoft, Earl of Worcester, now Constable of England, gave him short shrift, though he was spared the customary shame of wearing his arms reversed to his execution, because his ancestor had suffered severely for the sake of the King's grandfather, Richard, Earl of Cambridge. Instead, Tiptoft - more merciful than was his wont - allowed him his honours but, nevertheless, decreed his head should be exhibited, with those of many of the other rebels against the King's majesty, over London Bridge Gate.

By the end of July, the north was pacified and prospects for a lasting peace looked better than ever before. Leaving the new Earl of Northumberland to watch the Border, Warwick returned first to his estates and the castle from which he took his title and thence to London where, at the September Council he proposed a treaty of enduring peace should be signed with Louis of France. Further, he suggested that this should be cemented by the King's early marriage to Bona of Savoy, sister-in-law to Louis, and with the royal blood of France and Burgundy in her veins.

For much of the previous five years, England had alternately cultivated France and Burgundy, depending on whether York or Lancaster ruled, and whether kingdom or dukedom had the supremacy on the Continent. However, with good expectations of real peace in the northern counties at last, Richard Neville felt it was now time to finalise all his long, skilled, and often interrupted diplomacy, and to make a firm alliance with Louis and, necessarily therefore, to shed the less significant links - as Warwick now saw them - with Charles of Burgundy.

Other members of the Council agreed with Warwick that it was high time for the King, now 22 years of age, to take a wife and ensure the succession, and the King himself indicated that he was amenable to thoughts of marriage. Indeed, Edward told them, he had already decided on the lady he wished for his wife and when asked on whom his choice had fallen, he told them, the Lady Elizabeth Grey. His answer brought reactions varying from consternation to astonishment to sheer disbelief, but, through all, the young King kept his temper and eventually, to silence the growing volume of criticism, told his Council that the die was already cast. He had married Lady Elizabeth, nee Woodville, widow of a Lancastrian knight killed in the Wars with York, and mother of two sons of an age with the King's own younger brothers, on May Day, as he progressed northwards to help the Nevilles crush the Lancastrian-Scottish alliance.

Edward's revelation was a shattering blow to Warwick. For years he had cultivated his personal links with the French throne, started when he met Louis as Dauphin, in exile - ironically - at the court of Burgundy. Latterly, he had pursued more determinedly his goal of bringing England and France closer in friendship, a course which would eliminate support for the marauding Scots and for Lancaster at a stroke, and, to this end - and encouraged by Edward - had virtually pledged his King in marriage to the sister of the Queen of France. Now, thanks to the roving eye and lustful whim of a young, irresponsible monarch whom Warwick had installed on the throne of England, his plans were in ruins and the resulting loss of prestige at home and abroad would be difficult for the proud Premier Earl of England to bear.

However, for the present, there was no other course for Warwick than to appear to acquiesce in the King's decision and for some time the old friendly association continued, evidenced by the elevation of George Neville, Warwick's brother, and already Edward's Chancellor, to the vacant Archbishopric of York. But, with the new Queen now officially recognised and installed at Westminster, other marks of Royal favour began to fall thick and fast among her close relatives.

In October, her sister Margaret married the heir to the Arundel wealth and titles; in January, the Queen's youngest brother, John, married the wealthy Dowager Duchess of Norfolk who was old enough to be his grandmother; and over the next two years, Anne Woodville became wife to the heir of the Essex Earldom, sister Mary wed the heir of Lord Herbert who had stood with Edward at Mortimer's Cross, Eleanor married the heir of the Earl of Kent and Katherine became Duchess of Buckingham, greatly against the will of Henry Stafford, the youthful Duke, whose gift in marriage the King had casually and carelessly passed on to his own rapacious wife.

In May 1465, the formal Coronation of Queen Elizabeth took place but the Earl of Warwick, and his King, ensured that his presence would not be required. Instead, Richard Neville went to Burgundy and France, where his diplomatic expertise was unsuccessful in persuading the young, wilful heir to Burgundy, Charles the Rash, Count of Charolais, to renounce further support for Lancaster - Somerset and Exeter were pensioners at the Duke's court - but came off better in France, where Louis accepted his apology for the marriage debacle and agreed to give no help to Margaret of Anjou in return for Warwick's assurance that England would give no support to Burgundy or Brittany in their revolts against Louis' rule.

When Warwick returned to England, Edward professed himself well pleased with the Earl's success in gaining a truce of 18 months with Louis and, in February 1466, Warwick stood as Godfather to Edward's first-born, Elizabeth. A month later, however, Lord Mountjoy, a close friend of Warwick, was dismissed from office as Treasurer and replaced by Edward's father-in-law, Lord Rivers - he whom Edward, Warwick and the dead Salisbury had castigated as an upstart commoner years before in Calais - and the King made further recompense shortly afterwards by making Rivers an Earl.

An unkinder cut followed. George Neville, son of John, Lord Montagu and Earl of Northumberland, had been contracted to marry Anne, heiress to the rich estates of the (exiled) Duke of Exeter, but Elizabeth Woodville paid the Duchess four thousand marks to cancel the match and to marry her daughter to Thomas Grey, the Queen's elder son by her first marriage. The traditional Neville family policy of extending their power and influence through well-planned marriages had been pulled up short by the King's new relations, who were as prolific as, and even more grasping than, the Nevilles themselves.

They also had something the Earl of Warwick had lost - the ear of the King. Richard Neville recognised that his former influence over his young protege, Edward, Earl of March, was gone beyond hope of recovery, and, for the future, he could see only continuing growth in the influence of the parvenu Woodvilles, who would, stage by stage, usurp the rightful place of the Nevilles in the Kingdom. It was time for Richard Neville to start the making of a new King, and he thought he knew exactly the right young man for the position, and had exactly the right bait to catch him.

Engraving of Dunstanburgh Castle

(Geoffrey Wheeler)

CHAPTER FOURTEEN

"And yet they (Edward and Warwick) were accorded
diverse times; but they never loved together after ."
(Warkworth Chronicle)

In the two years following George Neville's enthronement as Archbishop of York on September 22nd 1465 - celebrated with a "gargantuan banquet" to mark the very height of Neville power in the north - relations between King Edward and his greatest Peer, Richard Neville, deteriorated steadily towards an inevitable breaking-point and the Earl commenced work on his secret master-plan to place a new King on England's throne. His selected instrument to ensure the continued dominance of the Neville family was George, Duke of Clarence, the elder of Edward's two surviving brothers, and the lure with which to attract him to Warwick's cause was his older daughter, Isabel, who at fifteen was a fitting match for the eighteen year old Clarence. As one of Warwick's two daughters, Isabel would in the natural course of time become "a lady richly left", bringing to her husband at least half of a mighty inheritance comprising the estates of Neville, Montacute, Despenser and Beauchamp. And, the damsel was 'passing fair', with the blood-royal through her descent from Joan Beaufort, and therefore, in every way, a fitting match for a Plantagenet Prince.

A further possibility along exactly the same lines offered itself through the long-term friendship between Warwick's second daughter, Anne and the youngest of Edward's brothers, Richard, Duke of Gloucester. Again, the two were well-matched in age and Anne's eventual inheritance would equal Isabel's, making her a desirable match for Richard, who had spent much of his later childhood and youth at Middleham, learning from the lordly Nevilles the dues and duties of a foremost Peer of the Realm.

To develop these prospects, Richard Neville invited the two brothers to spend a lengthy holiday with him and his family towards the end of 1466, during which the young people were thrown much together and George, in particular, was often in lengthy and private discussion with the Earl of Warwick. News of the visit soon reached the ears of the King, who sent for

Richard III

(Society of Artiquaries of London)

his two brothers to return to court, and when they came, he lectured them severely on their duty to him as their monarch, as well as the head of their family. Richard accepted his older brother's rebuke mildly, but Clarence - quite reasonably - pointed out that Isabel Neville would be an ideal match from every point of view and demanded good reasons why he should not continue to negotiate with Warwick. However, the victor of Towton was in no mood to argue with his young sibling and Edward forbade both brothers even from considering the possibility of marriage with the Neville family.

In the late Spring of the following year, the 18-month truce with the French was due to expire and Edward agreed with Warwick's advice that the Earl should go to Paris and there, in his King's name, negotiate a permanent peace with Louis of France. For some months prior to Warwick's departure, Edward had entertained embassies from Burgundy and from France, simultaneously but separately, and had enjoyed playing off one side of the French civil conflict against the other. However, such games have a finite time-span and the King agreed that Warwick should meet with Louis and discuss the terms of an enduring treaty of friendship between the two ancient enemies.

Unknown to Richard Neville, Edward had come to favour the Burgundian position, which would be more valuable to England's growing export trade in wool and woollen products - in which the King himself had a large financial interest - and which could be cemented more adequately through marriage between Charles of Charolais, heir to Burgundy, and Edward's sister Margaret. Thus it was that, when the Earl of Warwick returned to Sandwich towards the end of June, after long and apparently successful negotiations with Louis, enlivened with great celebrations in honour of, and many rich gifts to, the most distinguished English Lord living, he found his grand design in ruins. Burgundy's ambassadors - smugly self-satisfied - awaited ratification of their treaty, his own brother George was stripped of the Chancellorship with Robert Stillington, Bishop of Bath and Wells, installed in his place, and the Woodville faction was very clearly the new power behind the throne of the King of England.

Six weeks later, after entertaining appropriately, and bidding sad farewells to the French ambassadors as they embarked at Sandwich, Richard Neville, Earl of Warwick and Salisbury, erstwhile first adviser to the King, turned his horse's head northwards to Middleham. There, in his 'native' shire and the main seat of his power, he would start again on the reconstruction of the Realm into his own chosen design and this time there would be no room therein for Edward of March, nor for any low-born Woodvilles. Richard of Warwick would make another King.

Early in 1468, Edward sent for Warwick to join with him in a meeting of the Council, but the Earl would have none of it. He replied that never would he come again into Council, while his mortal enemies who were about the King's person - and he listed Earl Rivers, Lords Scales and Herbert and Sir John Woodville - remained there present. The close association between the two men who, together, had shaped the new kingdom was totally destroyed. It was clear to both that only one of them could now rule in the land and much English blood and treasure would be spent to decide who would be victor. Meantime, both were arch-dissemblers, whose first preference was to undo the other by subtle scheming rather than direct force and Warwick's clandestine moves soon started to show their effects.

In the same month he refused to join the King, Warwick was contacted by a captain of 300 archers named Robin, asking if it were time to be busy, but Richard Neville, told him to lie low and wait. Word would be sent when the time was right. Louis of France was equally busy with money and promises and a revolt appeared in the southwest led by Henry Courtney, heir to the Earl of Devon who fell at Towton, and Thomas Hungerford, whose father had died at Hexham. This was quickly put down by Lord Stafford, who was given the Devon title after executing the chief rebels at Salisbury. Jasper Tudor, Earl of Pembroke and half brother to Henry VI, with French help took Harlech and sacked Denbigh, but was soon defeated by Lord Herbert, who likewise took the Pembroke title while Tudor went back to hiding in the Welsh hills.

About Easter, George Neville, Archbishop of York and former Chancellor, met the King at the Royal request and from their increasingly warm discussions emerged a request to Richard Neville to resume his old friendship with Edward, who was in sore need of the Earl's wisdom, experience and advice on a projected invasion of France. Warwick, the great dissembler, agreed and met with the King again, even being reconciled - it seemed - with Lord Herbert, the new Earl of Pembroke, but exchanging no word with the Woodvilles.

On June 18, Warwick led the escort for Princess Margaret on the first part of her journey to marry Charles of Charolais, now Duke of Burgundy, and then returned to Middleham. From north Yorkshire, through agents, he stirred up troubles in Flanders, north Germany and Denmark and among the merchants of London, causing Edward's government problems and expense, while spending his time through to the early months of 1469 in apparent peaceable contentment. But, by April his grand design was ready, and Richard Neville moved decisively to retake control of England from the hands of the foolish, overly-young King wherein he had set it eight years before.

Bamburgh Castle, "the impregnable"

(Geoffrey Wheeler)

CHAPTER FIFTEEN

Treasons, stratagems and spoils.

𝕬s always, the Nevilles would work together to further the plans of their family-head and Warwick had the assurances of his brother George, awaiting the call in his Minster at York, his nephews, Lord Fitzhugh who would raise Richmondshire for the Bear and Ragged Staff and Henry Neville, heir to the Latimer title, his nephew by marriage Sir John Conyers of Hornby, and, importantly, the Bastard of Fauconberg, natural son of the great soldier of the family. Most important of all was Warwick's oldest surviving brother, John, Earl of Northumberland, the great general of the Kingmaker's armies, but he, though equally - and with better reason - detesting the Woodvilles, would not move against the King. On the other hand, his family ties would not permit him to betray Warwick's scheming to Edward. Caught between a rock and a hard place, John Neville could only wait and watch.

About the middle of April 1469, Warwick sailed from Sandwich to Calais taking with him his wife and his two daughters, his stated purpose being to visit his cousin Margaret in her new Duchy of Burgundy. While there, it would be natural for him to have talks with her husband, Charles, which would be more moderate in tone than their last meeting, and then on to Calais to stay with his old comrade-in-arms Lord Wenlock, inspect the fortifications, check the newly forming fleet, and await news from England of the developing discord, which he had ordered to begin as soon as his own absence on the King's business should disjoin himself from it.

By the end of June, much of north Yorkshire was up and 15,000 men led by Robert Huldyard under the nom de guerre Robin of Redesdale were at the gates of York with a string of written grievances reminiscent of the manifesto set out in Jack Cade's Kentish rebellion 20 years before. John Neville, in his capacity as Warden of the East March and with early intelligence of the rebellion, was in the city waiting with a strong force of well-armed men and he fell upon the rebels, routing them and beheading their leader. Loyalty still bound the Earl of Northumberland to his King's cause.

However, the spark struck by Huldyard soon had all the land twixt Humber and Tees ablaze and by the end of June, an army twice the size of the first was making a well-disciplined march south towards London, where their leaders would, they said, lay their grievances before the King himself. In the towns and villages they passed through, thoughtful hands pinned their well-written manifesto to the doors of local churches. At their head was a new 'Robin of Redesdale', an alias now assumed - so some said - by that most experienced of warriors, Lord Robert Ogle, hero of First St Albans and veteran of Towton, Constable of Norham, Lord of Redesdale, and long an adherent of the Middleham Nevilles.

On the failure of the first rising, Warwick had returned to England and was regularly in the King's company, advising, reassuring his Royal protege that all was being taken care of, everything was under control. John Neville would keep the north loyal and the new fleet would keep the seas clear of French intervention. Edward should make his long-intended pilgrimage to Walsingham at his leisure, and to this the King - ever willing to lose himself in pleasurable pursuits - gladly agreed. Accompanied only by his personal bodyguard of 200 archers, his brother Richard and Lord Hastings, and the leading menfolk of his wife's family, Earl Rivers and his two sons, Anthony, Lord Scales and Sir John Woodville, Edward began a stately royal progress through Norfolk.

By early July, however, increasingly disquieting reports on the rebellion's progress caused him to end his tour and to move towards Nottingham, where he summoned his chief supporters to rendezvous with him and to bring their men with them. Among those summoned were his brother, George of Clarence and the Earl of Warwick, but neither came to join the Royal Standard. Separately and quietly the two men had slipped away to Calais, where, on July 11th 1469 George Neville, Archbishop of York, had joined the Duke of Clarence in holy matrimony with Isabel, elder daughter of Richard Neville, Earl of Warwick and Salisbury. The Kingmaker's next monarch of England would be tied very firmly to the cause of the House of Neville and, with the last piece of his mosaic firmly in place, Warwick set sail for an England of which he intended to be undoubted ruler once more, and once for all.

With the men of Kent flocking to join them, Warwick and Clarence made the traditional detour to Canterbury, where they published the same manifesto that Robin of Redesdale's troops were propagating in the northern counties,

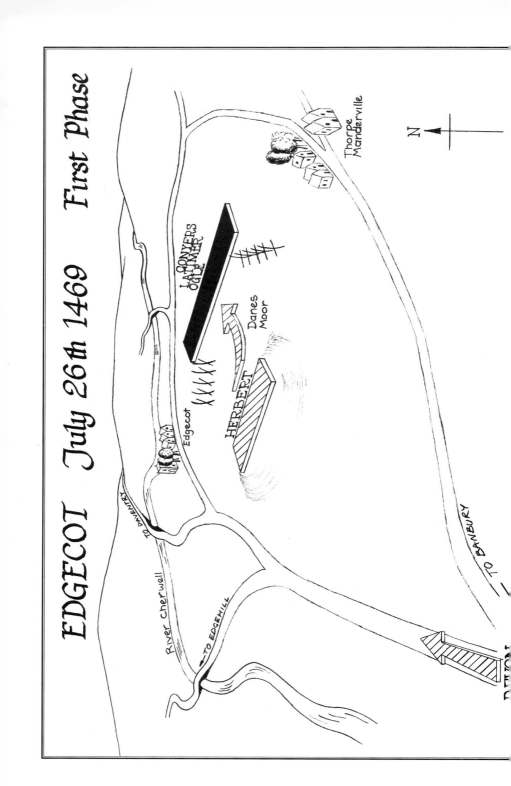

EDGECOT   July 26th 1469   First Phase

N

Thorpe Manderville

CONYERS
LATIMER
OGLE

Danes Moor

HERBERT

Edgecot

TO DAVENTRY

River Cherwell

←TO EDGEHILL

TO BANBURY

and which they said they would take with them to bring to the notice of the King. They then marched to London where the City Fathers needed no further prompting to throw open their gates to the popular, open-handed Earl of Warwick, and by July 20th, Richard Neville led an army many thousands strong towards St Albans on the way to link with Robin of Redesdale's host.

King Edward had not been idle and messengers to William Herbert, the new Earl of Pembroke, and to the equally newly installed Earl of Devon, had seen armies of more than 10,000 Welsh pikemen and over 5,000 West Country archers making their way with all possible expedition towards the rendezvous point of Nottingham. Here the King had collected a mixed body of troops, again numbering several thousand, and he waited urgently the arrival of his reinforcements from the west before deciding which of the two converging hostile forces to confront first. In the interim, he sent his Woodville relatives away when advised that his army was less likely to fight if they felt they were being used to protect the unpopular Rivers and his sons.

The northern army was the first to reach Nottinghamshire, but instead of moving to invest the county town as Edward expected, the rebels led by Redesdale, Conyers and Latimer, kept going south to Leicester, where they rested having interposed their force between the King and his Welsh reinforcement. The next day they moved on to Daventry and, learning that Pembroke's army was moving north towards them, the Yorkshiremen pushed forward again and the two armies met a few miles northeast of Banbury on open, hilly moorland near the hamlet of Edgecot; it was the 26th day of July, 1469.

Unhappily for the Welshmen, their leader Pembroke had had a furious row with the Earl of Devon on the previous evening, apparently over the billeting of their respective forces. The Welshmen had arrived first at Banbury and taken up all the available billets, which had meant Devon moving his contingent some six miles south to Deddington Castle, and the Westcountrymen were now following on well behind the main force, leaving Pembroke's pikemen short of numbers and devoid of the essential support of bowmen. When Pembroke realised he had run into a much larger opposing army from Yorkshire, he hurriedly drew his men up in a strong defensive formation on high ground to the south of, and commanding, an ideal battle site called Danes Moor. Messengers were sent spurring back to the laggardly Devon, and Herbert settled to await the onset from Robin of Redesdale's well-armed and armoured masses, hoping for time enough for Devon's archers to reach him.

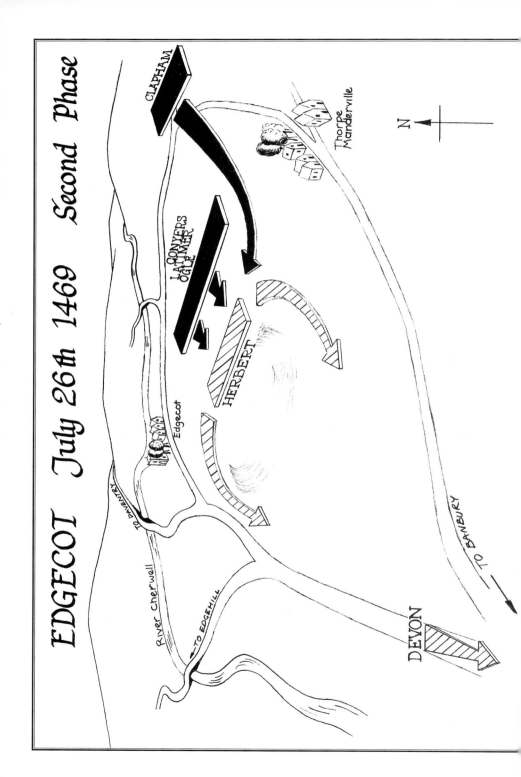

EDGECOT July 26th 1469 Second Phase

Ogle, Latimer and Conyers, however, did not keep him waiting long and their volleys of arrows and handgun missiles, which the Welshmen could not match, soon cut swathes through the ranks of Herbert's pikemen. Soon, Pembroke recognised - as Somerset had done at Towton - that he could not continue to stand on the high ground while his men were massacred at long range and his army moved downhill on to the plain where it was assailed by the waiting northcountry infantry. Nevertheless, their position partially protected by a branch of the Cherwell, the Welshmen stuck manfully to their task and beat off the initial attacks.

Latimer fell leading an early charge, while Ogle was carried away from the fighting sorely wounded and died later from the effects, but the Yorkshiremen would not be denied and returned again and again to the assault. Then, the deciding moment, the advance guard of Warwick's army led by a Towton veteran, John Clapham of Skipton, had been marching to the east of the conflict, heading northwards to join with their rebel comrades. Hearing the clangour and cries of battle from their left, they turned west and, unhappily for William Herbert, reached the action at exactly the critical moment for both sides. Assessing the position instantly - and probably with memories of Norfolk's intervention at Towton - Clapham and his men, with battlecries of "A Warwick, A Warwick", immediately launched themselves on the flank and rear of the tiring Welshmen, who broke and ran.

The briefly-titled Earl of Pembroke, William Herbert, divisional commander at Mortimer's Cross and Towton and ever-loyal to the House of York, was taken prisoner with his brother Richard and both were executed next day on the orders of the surviving rebel commander, Sir John Conyers, without courtesy of trial and, no doubt, at the behest of the Earl of Warwick. The surviving Welsh bore news of their defeat to the laggard Earl of Devon's force and all dissolved away to friendlier territory in the west and southwest. Edward's army, hearing from fleeing survivors of the disaster at Edgecot, likewise melted into the darkening evening and Richard Neville, who had arrived on the field in the aftermath of the battle, was content to let them go.

Warwick's only business now was with the King and while he moved on with his northern men towards Coventry, sending his Kentish men back to their homes, the Archbishop of York, George Neville, with a heavily armed escort set out towards Olney, where Edward, now with a mere handful of men-at-arms and archers, and accompanied only by his brother, Richard of Gloucester and his old friend William Hastings, awaited the Kingmaker's pleasure.

Edward and Richard Neville met again on the last day of July and the King was not slow to exercise his charm on his cousins and his brother, George of Clarence. Whatever the Earl of Warwick desired should be done and if formal Royal assent were required it would be given immediately. The first rush of proclamations implementing Warwick's policies and signed with Edward's seal went out on August 2nd, though he was not asked to countersign the death warrants for Earl Rivers and John Woodville. The pair had been taken at Chepstow on the Severn and were forwarded to Warwick for judgement. This they had and were beheaded on August 12th at Coventry. Days later came news that the Earl of Devon had fallen into the hands of retainers of the Courtenays - the Lancastrian holders of the Devon title - and had received similarly short shrift from them.

The board, for the time being at least, was swept clean. Warwick had a compliant King firmly in his grasp, his main enemies were dead or flown, his word was law. Let Gloucester and Hastings try to rebuild the King's party, and Margaret of Burgundy's gold and agents stir the London mob on her brother's behalf, Richard Neville had undivided power at last and, through Clarence, the instrument, perhaps, to make the settlement permanent. Only Edward's life stood between Richard Neville and the rule over England, but - he hesitated. The King was in Warwick Castle, where he was more secure than at Coventry and, to make assurance doubly sure, Warwick would move him to his great Keep at Middleham, heart of the Neville power. Then he would have time to think on what more might be done.

CHAPTER SIXTEEN

"The King himself hath good language of Clarence and Warwick...but his household men have other language"
(Paston Letters)

To legitimise his assumption of power, Warwick needed the endorsement of Parliament and he wasted no time in using the King's seal to call an assembly on September 20, to be held not at Westminster, but in the Neville stronghold of York. However, this project was swiftly overtaken by events, for in the absence of any legalised authority, the Kingdom was rapidly degenerating into anarchy. Old feuds were being revived and settled in most parts of the land; in London the mob - ever a potent weapon of Richard Neville - was stirring : to the victors the spoils, pillage the rich, drive out the Flemings. The citizenry had played their part in Warwick's triumph, now pay-day had come.

Warwick sent Clarence and his Archbishop brother, George, to the capital to calm things, but they had little success, nor did the messengers sent to separate the Duke of Norfolk and the Pastons in East Anglia, or the Talbots from the Berkeleys in the West country. The final straw arrived when Humphrey Neville - former defender of Bamburgh Castle and would-be ambusher of John Neville - took advantage of the growing chaos to launch across the Border a new revolt in favour of Lancaster. With bad news from all points of the compass and with the men of Robin of Redesdale unwilling to answer a further call to arms so soon, Richard Neville had little option but to ask Edward for his Royal support in raising men.

Recognising that his moment of recovery had come, the King agreed very willingly to support his cousin's legitimate efforts to bring peace again to the Realm, provided only that he was permitted a little more personal liberty. Indeed, he felt he could aid Warwick better if he were able to make a progress to York and encourage the townspeople to support the Earl against Sir Humphrey's revolt, even perhaps, to take up residence in his royal castle at Pontefract, so all his people would recognise that he stayed in Yorkshire of his own free will. Richard Neville grudgingly, but with no alternative immediately in view, agreed and with Edward's open backing, recruits flocked to the banners of Montagu and Warwick. With a powerful force behind him, John Neville moved quickly north and swept the Scots and Lancastrian exiles away back over the Border, giving the vanquished no quarter and returning in triumph to York with Sir Humphrey Neville as his prisoner. This time, Edward's patience had been tried once too often and, on September 29th, Humphrey Neville was publicly executed in York in the King's presence.

A week after his return to Pontefract, Richard of Gloucester with Hastings and other Lords of Edward's court appeared at the castle. They brought with them a large, heavily armed force which was swelled by many of the triumphant men-at-arms of John Neville, Earl of Northumberland, who again made clear his support for his cousin, the King. Surprised by this subtle King's gambit, Warwick had no other course but to agree with Edward's smiling indication that he felt it was time for him to return to his capital and he would be leaving with all his Lords that very day to deal with the pressing business which had arisen in his unexpectedly long absence.

Edward's brief imprisonment was at an end, Monarch and Chief Subject resumed their respective roles in the Kingdom, at least to all outside appearances. But to both men, it was now clear that not only could they not rule this land happily and successfully together, it was no longer possible even for both of them to live within the same Kingdom. Edward had parted from Warwick cheerfully and graciously, full of his usual charm and amiability, but he now knew that while the Kingmaker lived, no crowned head of England could ever lie easily in its bed. From that moment, Richard Neville was a man marked for death. Nor, for his part, was Warwick deceived by the display of light-hearted amity from his erstwhile protege and prisoner. He knew now he would only ever rule the land through his son-in-law, George of Clarence and that desirable consummation could only arise were the present King to be removed - permanently. When next Edward Plantagenet fell into the hands of Richard Neville, there would be no second Pontefract.

In the remaining months of 1469, following his return to London, Edward progressively erased the gains and advantages which Richard Neville had secured during his period as de facto Ruler of England. The King lost little time in dismissing Sir John Langstrother from the post of Treasurer, an appointment forced on him by Warwick, and of relieving the Earl himself of those Offices in south Wales which Neville had taken over from the dead Lord Herbert, Earl of Pembroke, and which the King now passed on to his brother, Richard of Gloucester. Anthony Woodville, the most senior male of the family to escape Warwick's wrath after Edgecot, appeared again at Westminster with his father's title of Earl Rivers, while the Earl of Warwick and George of Clarence found they were no longer included in summonses to court and their humbler supporters lost the lucrative posts in governance which the Nevilles had given them.

At the end of October, Edward made his first overt move to restore power in the northeast to the Percies of Alnwick, the obvious counter-weight to the Nevilles. Young Henry Percy, heir to the Earldom lost by his father, along with his life, at Towton eight years before, was released from the Tower on surety of future loyalty. In November, John Neville was advised of the impending loss of his Earldom by Edward and told he would be recompensed by the betrothal of his son, George, who had previously been disappointed of marriage with the Exeter heiress through the machinations of Elizabeth Woodville, to Edward's oldest child, and current heir, Elizabeth. George would be given further distinction by being created Duke of Bedford and John Neville would receive financial compensation for the loss of the Percy estates through the grant of lands in Devon, formerly held by the attainted Courtenays.

On March 1st, 1470, Henry Percy recovered his Earldom and while John Neville was to be compensated for the pecuniary losses involved, and created Marquis Montagu with his son married to the King's daughter, there was no such recompense for Warwick and Clarence who had suffered associated losses in Yorkshire and Cumberland. Indeed, in January, Edward had also taken the first steps towards the restoration of the Dacre barony, which had likewise been vacant since Towton, and which would further neutralise Richard Neville's hegemony in the north. The Earl of Warwick sensed his power being whittled away, piece by piece, sliver by sliver, and knew he must counter-attack before he was terminally weakened.

As always, Warwick favoured the indirect approach and developed a plan virtually identical in essence to the stratagem by which he had snared the King in the previous year. He would use supporters to raise apparent rebellion in one part of the country, enlist levies ostensibly to aid Edward in putting down the rebels and then catch the King between the supposedly opposing forces. The scheme had worked to perfection before, but Warwick had made one vital mistake, he had underrated his opponent. Edward, whatever his other shortcomings, had not achieved the throne through blind stupidity and he would not be caught twice in the same net.

Alnwick Castle, Northumberland

(Geoffrey Wheeler)

CHAPTER SEVENTEEN

"The great rising was (because) the king was coming with great power (to) hang and draw great number of the commons..."
(Bentley, Excerpta Historica.)

Warwick's opening gambit was through Lord Richard Welles, who was related by marriage to the Earl's liegeman Sir James Strangways, and who had a long-standing feud with Sir Thomas Burgh of Gainsborough. Sir Thomas was Edward's chief supporter in Lincolnshire and any attack on him would be met by and with the King's own force. By February, all was prepared, Richard Neville was at Warwick Castle, Clarence in London keeping a close watch on the King, and without warning, "riotous bands" led by Sir Robert Welles, son and heir to Lord Richard, moved through the county and attacked and plundered Thomas Burgh's manor house and estates. At the same time, the rioters raised the familiar complaints of ill government and some called for restoration of Henry VI to his former throne.

Recognising the seriousness of this latest challenge to his authority, Edward immediately summoned Lord Welles with his brother-in-law Sir Thomas Dymmock to Westminster to account for their actions. The two men obeyed the summons, disclaiming involvement in the actions of Robert Welles, and were readily absolved by the King but, despite the safe-conducts he had sent to them, were kept in safe-custody as a potential bargaining chip should the need for such arise. Meantime, Edward sent out commissions of array to raise sufficient force to put down the rising, among which were documents empowering Richard Neville and George of Clarence to raise levies for the King in Warwickshire and Worcestershire.

Warwick's scheme was maturing exactly as he had planned and, while assuring the King of his loyalty and that he would join him as summoned at Grantham on March 12th, he sent messages of encouragement to Sir Robert Welles, instructing him to by-pass the King's army as it moved into Lincolnshire and join himself and Clarence on the same date at Leicester. Thus, their united stronger force would stand between the King and his capital

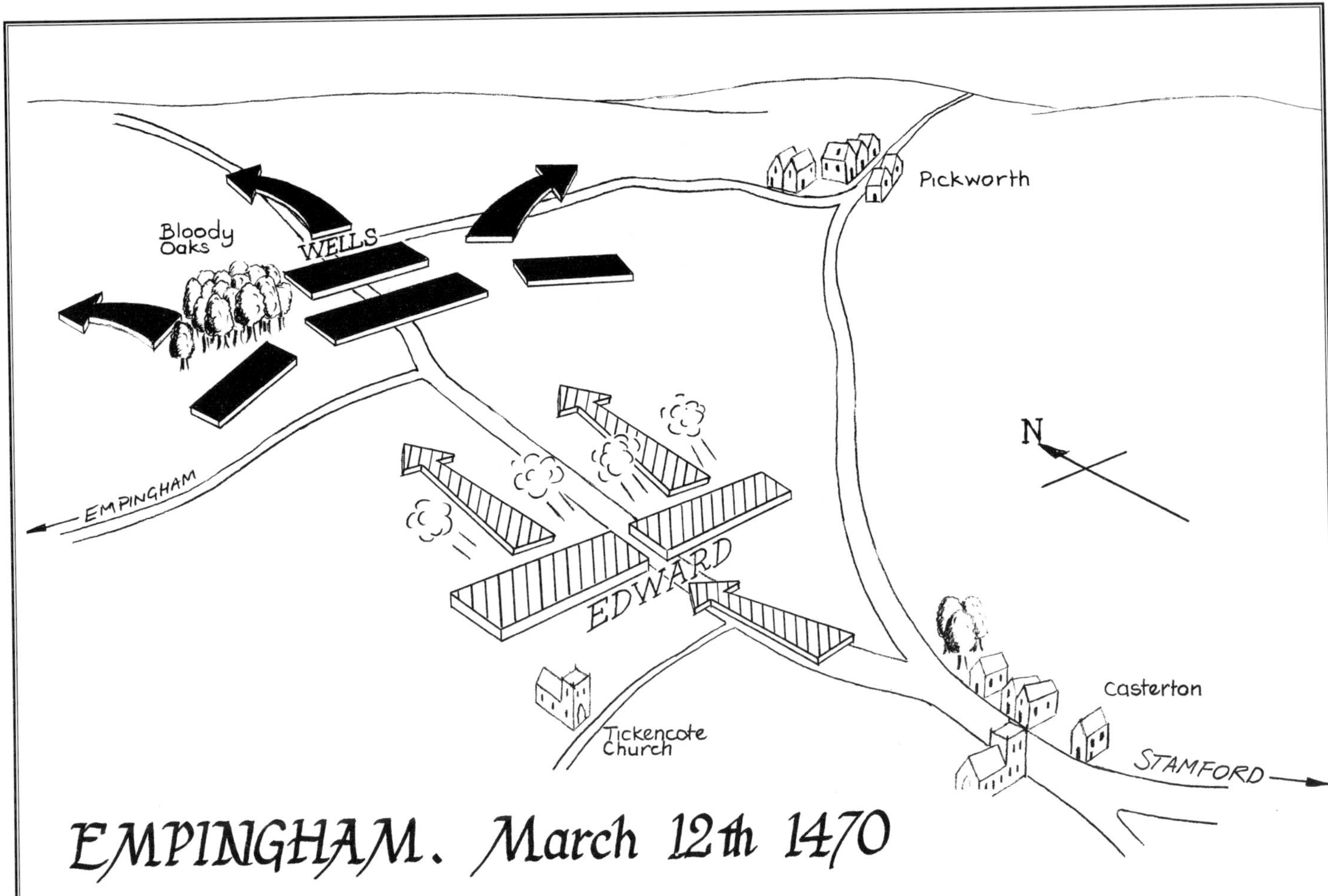

Bloody Oaks
WELLS
Pickworth
EMPINGHAM
N
EDWARD
Tickencote Church
Casterton
STAMFORD
EMPINGHAM. March 12th 1470

and again Edward would be at Warwick's disposal and, this time, his shrift would be short indeed. Unhappily for Richard Neville and the Lincolnshire rebels, Edward was marching to a different drum and, accurately guessing Warwick's intentions, had left London early on March 6th and reached Stamford five days later with a very strong force at his back.

The King's scouts located the rebel force some five miles to the northwest and Edward sent heralds summoning Sir Robert Welles to surrender himself on pain of his father's life. The rebel leader on hearing the king's demand, supported as it was by a heart-rending plea from his aged father, sent a message to Warwick that he had no recourse but to move immediately on Edward's army to save his father's life. And so it was that on Monday, March 12th, instead of joining Warwick as planned at Leicester, Welles met Edward at the village of Empingham near Stamford and, when he refused the King's command to disperse, saw his father and his uncle, Sir Thomas Dymmock, beheaded before the two armies.

This ruthless action caused some panic within the rebel ranks, which immediately after were badly cut up by Edward's artillery barrage The following charge of Edward's heavy cavalry scattered the men of Lincolnshire who fled before this onset, with many dying in the following pursuit. A copse immediately behind the rebel line was given the name, Bloody Oaks, to commemorate the killing that was done there and, beyond the trees, the open ground was littered with cast-off surcoats of the fleeing rebels to such a degree that it was known ever after as Lose-coat Field.

Welles was captured at Doncaster days later and, after severe questioning, suffered the immediate decapitation decreed by the triumphant King, who then turned his mind to dealing with the real villains of the piece. Warwick and Clarence had moved to Chesterfield and were anxiously awaiting reinforcement from north Yorkshire, where Sir John Conyers, the survivor of Edgecot, with Lords Scrope and Fitzwalter, was raising men in support of Warwick's master plan. However, news of Lose-coat Field was not slow to reach them and was followed quickly by Edward's proclamation of his brother, George of Clarence, and Richard Neville, Earl of Warwick, to be traitors as witnessed by Sir Robert Welles in his dying confession, and prohibiting any Lord or knight from raising armed levies without the express permission of the King.

These tidings were enough to ensure that Yorkshire remained quiet, waiting a clearer report on how their Earl's position stood against the King's and, when Edward arrived at York on March 21st to reprovision his army, Conyers, Scrope and Fitzwalter, with their chief lieutenants, appeared before him and offered their submission to his grace and mercy. This, the King having larger fish to fry, they received and Edward made preparations to pursue the chief traitors, who had moved to Neville's castle at Warwick, where they collected their families and then made for the south coast and the, by now, traditional sanctuary of Calais.

Warwick counted on using Calais as a secure base from which to make a further sortie on England, after a new master-plan had been developed, and was disagreeably surprised by his reception as he attempted to enter the harbour. The Captain whom Warwick had installed to keep the port safely loyal to the Neville cause was Lord John Wenlock, one of the great coat-turners of his generation, who had received messages from the King, mere hours before the Earl's arrival, forbidding him to permit the Nevilles to land, on peril of his life. Accordingly Wenlock, rather than arranging welcoming festivities, ordered his troops to man their batteries and greeted Warwick with volleys of shot from the great cannon.

Disconcerted, Warwick withdrew and lay off Calais for some days, while his daughter Isabel bore Clarence his first child, a son but unhappily born dead, on which news, Wenlock sent supplies of wine to aid the Duchess's recovery together with secret messages to Richard Neville promising a fairer welcome next time, but urging patience meanwhile. Warwick had little option but to accept this advice and he withdrew his small fleet to Honfleur and anchored there at the beginning of May. Louis did not immediately rush to welcome him, but sent his Secretary, du Plessis, and High Admiral, the Bastard of Bourbon, in his stead with diplomatic greetings and assurances of supply. Knowing his man, Warwick possessed himself in patience to await the summons from Louis of France which he knew must surely come. The Spider King would not long neglect so promising an opportunity to plot harm for Edward of England, the young, giant monarch whose shadow still fell heavily across the Channel and deep into France.

With Warwick out of the way, at least for the time being, Edward turned his thoughts to northern England and looked for ways to reduce the power of the Nevilles. Immediately, he did little to disturb the normal pattern of life on

Warwick's own estates, though he restored Barnard Castle to the Bishop of Durham, still the Laurence Booth installed 13 years earlier by Margaret of Anjou to diminish Neville power, and gave custody of young Richard Neville, heir to the Latimer estates, to Thomas Bourchier, Archbishop of Canterbury. The latter measure did not work out exactly as planned since custody of the boy was secretly maintained by Lord Fitzhugh, Richard of Warwick's brother-in-law.

However, the King was more successful in restoring the power of the Percies in Northumberland. Having formally bestowed the Earldom on Henry Percy, during his stay in York, Edward also gave him back the traditional family title of Warden of the East March, and thus completely eliminated the Neville power northeast of the Yorkshire border. John Neville was compensated for his displacement with his higher title, Marquess Montagu, lands in the southwest of equivalent value to those returned to Percy, and the promise of marital alliance with the King's own family.

Obsessed with the urgent need to curb Warwick's power while the opportunity existed, Edward pushed his new ordering of affairs below the Scottish Border with all speed and, in his haste, omitted to make sure that John Neville, his ever-loyal, hard-fighting, taciturn cousin, was happy with the massive, forced changes in his affairs. It was a mistake which would cost Edward dearly in short course.

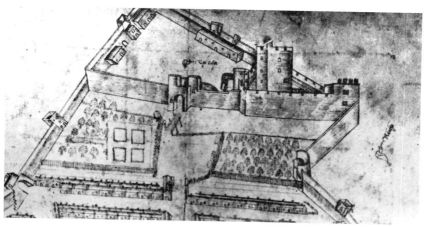

Carlisle Castle, from an Elizabethan Plan.
(Geoffrey Wheeler)

103

CHAPTER EIGHTEEN

"...by the mean of the King of France, the said Earl of Warwick purchased a pardon of the Queen Margaret and of her son..."
(Chronicles of the White Rose)

By the beginning of June, Louis was more than ready to talk with Richard Neville, whose regular piratical descents on the coast and commerce of Burgundy were causing near apoplexy on the part of the choleric Duke Charles. It was essential for the French King to find a more-rewarding outlet for the energies of the exiled Earl and his seafarers, and one which would also be of benefit to France. A difficult dilemma to solve, but the Spider King thought he might just have an answer, and one which could kill several birds with a single cast.

In the early days of June, Louis invited Warwick and Clarence to visit him in the Royal castle of Amboise and while entertaining them extravagantly, he confided his plans to the two English Lords. In essence, Louis proposed that Warwick and Margaret of Anjou and her son, Edward Prince of Wales, should be reconciled; that, financed by French gold, Richard Neville should return to England and there set King Henry VI back on his throne; and that Edward of Lancaster should marry Warwick's younger daughter Anne, thus permanently uniting the Houses of Neville and Plantagenet of Lancaster. In return for Louis' help, there would be a permanent treaty of peace between France and England and the two countries would unite to defeat Burgundy's short-tempered young ruler and bring him to lasting obedience to his French overlord.

On June 12th, Warwick and the disappointed Clarence, who had seen his own dreams of the English throne destroyed at Amboise, rode to Vendome to await further news from Louis. The only snag with the Spider's brilliant scheme was that Margaret of Anjou had not yet been told of it and both men thought it best for Louis to be alone with her, when he first divulged his idea. They were right. Queen Margaret's initial reaction was one of furious rejection. Richard Neville was the chief cause of all the misfortunes which had befallen her, her husband and her son; he had called her an adulteress and her son a bastard; never, never, would she join forces with this evil man.

But, slowly, slowly, the King of France talked her round to his point of view. Without Warwick's aid Margaret might never return to rule England, her son's birthright would be lost beyond recall. Above all else, Margaret had to get rid of the usurper Edward and his family, to seat her husband again in his rightful place, and who was more likely to be able to help her to this objective than the most powerful Lord in all England? And, after Edward was dead, and Margaret and Henry ruled again, who knew what 'fitting reward' might be arranged for Richard Neville, whose vast estate would, of course, descend to his daughter - and her husband.

Gradually, gradually, the softly-spoken arguments of the King of France, supported by Margaret's Chancellor, Sir John Fortescue, and most subtly by her chaplain/clerk, John Morton, wore down her resistance and finally she agreed on all points. She made only two unalterable reservations : Richard Neville must beg her pardon for all his offences against her and her House, publicly on bended knee, and this humiliation must be repeated in Westminster after the reconquest was accomplished; furthermore, she and her son would come to England only when Lancastrian rule had been safely and securely re-established. The Earl of Warwick alone must take all the risks involved in facing and defeating Edward Plantagenet, in order to ensure the indisputable restoration of England's true Queen.

In a later age, a King of France would declare that Paris was worth a mass and, for Richard Neville, England was worth a bending of the knee. On July 22nd, at Angers, the Earl of Warwick and Salisbury, greatest Lord in England, knelt humbly before the penniless Queen who had ordered his father's death, and besought forgiveness for the wrongs he had done her and her family. Margaret kept him in suspense for 15 minutes before accepting his apologies, and even then contrasted her icy manner to Warwick by effusively greeting his companion, John de Vere, Earl of Oxford, whose family had suffered much in the cause of Lancaster.

Over the next three days, a detailed agreement was hammered out by which Louis would support Margaret and her train in royal style - likewise Neville's womenfolk - until their return to England. Jasper Tudor and John de Vere, Warwick's brother-in-law, would accompany the Kingmaker to England, as would the Parson of Blokesworth, John Morton, who would keep a watching brief for his Angevin mistress. Clarence would also return with Warwick and would receive all his former estates and the still-larger holdings of the Duchy of York when the rule of Henry was restored. Further, in the event that Edward of Lancaster and Anne Neville died childless, Clarence would be acknowledged heir to the throne. One way or another, Richard Neville's blood-line would one day sit on the throne of England, rulers by right of birth as well as by strength of arm and intellect.

The only remaining obstacle was Edward IV of England and Richard Neville had already started the moves which would unseat the King he had made, and this time, permanently. Messengers sped from Warwick at his base in Valognes to his main seat of power in northern England; the heirs of Robin of Redesdale were being summoned again to their duties by the Master of Middleham.

The ink was barely dry on the secret Treaty of Angers, when Henry Fitzhugh, Warwick's brother-in-law, raised all Richmondshire - but for Warwick rather than against the King - and the Yorkshiremen were joined immediately by Cumbrian levies raised by Richard Salkeld of Corby in his capacity as Constable of Carlisle. The conspiracy was orchestrated once more by the faithful Sir John Conyers, Steward of Middleham, and many of the local gentry brought their levies to join the main band. Shortly, several thousand well-armed and disciplined northerners were assembled and reconnoitred east and northwards into Percy lands and probed towards the south, but, in the main, seemed content to hold their position, as though awaiting the arrival of their designated leader.

Edward was soon aware of the stirrings in his northern counties and by August 5th had concluded that urgent, decisive action was required. He raised the southern levies and with his brother Richard of Gloucester, Lords Hastings and Scales and many other Barons, marched north, reaching Ripon on August 14th. And now, such was the force of his reputation as a warrior-king, that the rebellion died down immediately and, in line with his normal policy, Edward was issuing pardons to penitent rebels by early September. However, convinced that Richard Neville would be returning to his native heath before long, the King stayed on in the north, as Warwick had assumed he would, and was thus over 300 miles distant, when the Earl landed without opposition at Dartmouth on September 25th, 1470.

The southwestern counties of England were ever strong for Lancaster and when Warwick and Clarence, accompanied as they were by Lancastrian Lords and gentlemen, led by the Earls of Oxford and Pembroke, issued their joint proclamation that they came to restore Henry, the rightful King, to his throne, recruits flocked to their banners. Knowing time was of the essence, Richard Neville pressed northeastwards as quickly as his growing army could move, joining with Talbot, Earl of Shrewsbury and another Neville brother-in-law, Lord Thomas Stanley en route to Coventry, where Warwick arrived leading an army reported as 30,000 men. Here he halted to organise and resupply his force, to await the King's next move, and to see the effect of his own, imminent coup de grace.

Edward, from his base at York had turned his army southwards as soon as news of Warwick's return reached him, and had sent to Montagu, who was lying at Pontefract with the bulk of the Yorkist forces, to join him at Doncaster with all his men. Montagu sent word that he would meet Edward as ordered, but, on the way to the Don crossing, he had word from his brother of his arrival at Coventry with a vastly superior army of Lancastrians, all eager to wipe out the memories of ten years of Yorkist supremacy. John Neville was caught again between his older brother's driving ambition and his demand for family loyalty, and his oath to a King whom he had served faithfully and well and from whom he had scant reward for his efforts in the end. If Edward had kept faith with him, there can be little doubt that Montagu would have stayed loyal to his King. As it was, with bitter memories of the loss of his Earldom and his lands in the north still fresh in his mind, John Neville had no stomach to engage his men in a hard and bloody contest with a vastly superior army, led by his brother. Instead, he rode among his troops telling them that, if they followed him, he would lead them against Edward the next day.

The vast majority of Montagu's army agreed to follow him and when the King had word that his comparatively small force was ensnared between the oncoming Montagu and the waiting Warwick, he fled accompanied only by Richard of Gloucester, William Hastings, his brother-in-law Earl Rivers, and a handful of guards. On October 2nd, the party sailed from King's Lynn in Norfolk, making for the uncertain sanctuary offered by Burgundy. Richard Neville could now turn all his attention to the seat of power in London, where the overthrow of the King had brought the customary anarchy in its wake.

George Neville, Archbishop of York, reached the capital with a small, but well-armed force and took over the Tower on October 5th. On the following day, Richard Neville and George of Clarence, still accompanied by Thomas, Lord Stanley and John Talbot, Earl of Shrewsbury, reached London with their combined forces and Warwick went immediately to make his obeisance to the restored King Henry. The following week, the Earl rode with his newly-recreated Monarch to the cathedral of St Paul's to give thanks for the Royal restoration and then settled immediately into his familiar Office, which he saw as giving England the governance which he deemed was needed.

CHAPTER NINETEEN

"...and wrote in all his writs and other records 'in the forty-ninth year of the reign of King Henry and in the first of the restoration of his royal power'..."

(Warkworth Chronicle.)

Although Henry VI was nominally restored as ruler of England, the real power was in the firm grasp of Richard Neville. He took upon himself the new title of King's Lieutenant of the Realm - nominating for appearances' sake Clarence and Pembroke as associates - and also resumed his former Offices as Captain of Calais and Great Chamberlain. His brother George was reinstated as Chancellor and Sir John Langstrother, Prior of the Hospitallers, as Treasurer. For his brother John, rewards were more slender. Montagu was simply restored to his former Office of Warden of the East March and given Lordship of the Manor of Wressle again, a single crumb from the Percy estate, which, for a brief, idyllic space, had been his own Earldom.

He was sent north to watch the Border and the Yorkshire coast, but only after Warwick had required him to make public apology before the first Parliament of the new reign for his previous Yorkist sympathies. If Warwick could humble himself in the family interest, there was no reason why his younger brother should not do the same. Back in his native county, Montagu based himself at Pontefract again, as the most convenient site from which to cover threats from north or east and, no doubt, had time to reflect on the wisdom of choosing Warwick and Lancaster over York. A brief moment would come when he would have an opportunity to change his mind, but he was a man set in his ways, already bearing many scars, physical and otherwise, from loyalty to his Neville family and to York. When the two main influences in one's life divided, so disastrously and so finally, what future could there be with either for a fighting-man of simple loyalties ?

Within Warwick's new Council, there was equally little place for the Lords whose families had been constant in their support for Lancaster. Talbot,

Earl of Shrewsbury and de Vere, Earl of Oxford were able to busy themselves on their own lands, ensuring support from their tenants for King Henry's return to the throne, and Courtenay of Devon found ample work to occupy him in reclaiming the loyalty of his people following his return from exile. Jasper Tudor, restored Earl of Pembroke, whose main duty following the return had been to ensure peace in the Welsh Marches, found time now to come to Westminster and to bring with him young Henry Tudor, his nephew and only son of Margaret Beaufort, to plead for the grant of his father's title of Earl of Richmond. In this, Richard Neville was unable to oblige him, since the Earldom in question was already adopted by George of Clarence, who had sacrificed much for the advancement of Warwick's schemes.

Jasper tried to get the ear of his half-brother, Henry, but the King was ever at his devotions and left the rule of the Kingdom entirely to Richard Neville. After two weeks of fruitless waiting, the Tudors returned to Wales taking with them only a commission to salvage what they might from the former estates of Lord William Herbert, lately Earl of Pembroke. Their time would come, but not until three Kings of England and thousands more of their subjects had died, and another 15 years had passed.

During the November Parliament, the formalities necessary to establish the return of Lancastrian rule under the Earl of Warwick occupied most of the proceedings. Former attainders against Lancastrian nobles, notably those of Edmund Beaufort, Duke of Somerset and Henry Holland, Duke of Exeter, were reversed, and similar proscriptions against the usurper, Edward Duke of York, and his brother, Richard Duke of Gloucester, were substituted. Warwick's key appointments were ratified and provision was made for the succession of George of Clarence in the event of the Lancastrian line failing. Most importantly, a treaty of peace and friendship with France was agreed for 12 years, which bound England to an alliance with Louis of France against Charles, Duke of Burgundy.

This last act was not supported by the merchants and guilds because it harmed the wool export trade so essential to the country's economic well-being, nor did it find favour among the people generally, still sore over the loss of England's former demesne in Normandy and Gascony. But, for the Earl of Warwick and Salisbury, it was the necessary price for the French support so vital to his restoration and to his policy, and he must - and he would - pay it willingly, gladly, to put the final seal on recovery of his dominion over English land, and assure his place in History as the greatest Neville of all.

Edward, whose Queen - once more within the Abbey's sanctuary - had presented him with his first son on November 2nd, and thereby given him increased incentive to take back his Kingdom, was already plotting his return. His brother-in-law, Charles of Burgundy, was proving singularly unhelpful, but Edward felt that developing events would inevitably change his attitude for the better and knew he could rely on his sister Margaret's untiring advocacy of his cause with her husband in the interim. Through Margaret, he also resumed contact with his brother George of Clarence, who grew increasingly disappointed with his lot in the new scheme of things and who indicated to Edward that he would certainly rejoin him, with all the men he could muster, once his brother set foot again in England.

The Treaty with the King of France was ratified in a short Parliament in February, 1471 and Louis, who had started preparatory moves against Burgundy in the late Autumn of the previous year, following Warwick's successful resumption of power, was not slow to recommence hostilities with Burgundy and to demand that England should play its part in the campaign. Warwick was short of funds, there was nothing in the state coffers and his own treasure was badly depleted by the necessary expenses incurred during his exile and return, but he had scraped together a respectable-sized force and awaited only the return of his erstwhile enemy, Margaret of Anjou, to take the burden of governing the realm before he made sail again for Calais.

But Queen Margaret was still fearful of trusting her life and her future fortune to the Earl of Warwick. Again and again she sent word that she was on the verge of returning, only to draw back at the last moment, and Richard Neville must again write to the King of France that he could not - dare not - leave the Kingdom in hands less safe than Margaret's, but that he would personally lead the English expeditionary force across the Channel to aid Louis, the moment that the governance of his country was assured.

Still Margaret and her son did not come, and the weather had turned foul with the wind set strongly from the northwest, keeping the French ships locked in their harbours, the one consolation being that the same wind would keep Edward firmly fastened likewise in the ports of Burgundy. And then, towards the middle of March, the wind veered eastwards and Warwick again prepared to move his compact force out of London towards Sandwich and Calais. His plans, however, were abruptly changed by the arrival of a mud-spattered rider from Norfolk, with news of the sighting of a fleet, flaunting Yorkist banners and heading north past Cromer.

Edward's patient wait for Charles of Burgundy's views to change had been rewarded. Louis' moves on the Somme fortresses and a constant flow of reports from Burgundy's spies at the French Court on the imminent arrival of Warwick's forces in support had forced the Duke's hand. Grudgingly still, he had loaned Edward men and money, with which, in ships supplied by Warwick's sworn enemies, the Hanse merchants, the Yorkist King was returning to England. On March 14th 1471, with around 2,000 men and accompanied by his brother Richard and his trusty friend Lord William Hastings, Edward landed - like Henry Bolingbroke 70 years before him - in the tiny port of Ravenspur at the mouth of the Humber.

Warwick was already moving northwards when this news reached him, gathering men and sending out urgent summonses to friends and to his new Lancastrian allies to rally to him at Coventry. Among the messages, he sent to John Neville at Pontefract telling him that York's giant champion had returned and that he must do his utmost to delay Edward's inevitable movement southwards to London. His brother must give Warwick time to gather a great army with which to settle accounts with Edward, once and for all. When he read this, Montagu nodded his head slowly and grimly, and wondered how many of Percy's men would obey the summons of a Neville. Still, he could but try.

Arms and signature of William, Lord Hastings

112

CHAPTER TWENTY

*"The king determined...to say that his intent...was only to claim
to be Duke of York and to have the inheritance that he was
born unto, and none other."*
[Arrivall of King Edward IV]

After reassembling his small forces which had been scattered in a storm prior to landing, Edward made his way along the Humber and up the Ouse to York, where he proclaimed that he came only for his own and had no more thoughts of kingship. Then, having recruited more men, he progressed southwards towards his family's castle at Wakefield, where his father and nearest brother had died ten years earlier and, moving south again, sent a heavy flank guard to the east of his line of march, lest John Neville should move to the attack from Pontefract. But he and his army successfully passed this point of potential crisis, the Marquess Montagu had too few men, he felt, to risk confronting Edward and he let the King pass, unopposed, and then followed slowly in his wake towards Coventry. Let his brother Richard strike the final fatal blow against York.

As Edward progressed further and further southwards, so did his cause appear stronger and opponents, actual and potential, became progressively less ready to strike at him. He halted to rest his troops at Nottingham and there received news that John de Vere, Earl of Oxford and Henry Holland, Duke of Exeter had reached Newark, a few miles to his northeast. Montagu continued to follow him some miles further to the north and Warwick's main force was south of him at Coventry and moving up towards Leicester. Unless he took immediate action, Edward risked being trapped between three Lancastrian armies and crushed utterly.

Always at his most decisive when disaster threatened, Edward moved quickly against the nearest of his foes, Oxford and Exeter, making a swift thrust through the night towards Newark. The Lancastrians were alarmed by a clash of pickets as Edward's vanguard ran into Oxford's sentries and, panicking, the whole force packed as much gear as came immediately to hand and fled southwards to link with Warwick. When they joined with Richard

Neville on the road south of Leicester, he - ever-cautious - decided the best course was to retreat back to his starting point and give the enlarged army time to settle again, protected by Coventry's stout walls.

Edward had pursued Oxford south past Leicester and soon came with his whole force to the barred gates of Coventry, with the Bear and Ragged Staff and the red Neville saltire banners fluttering from the town's walls. Here he drew his army up in battle order and awaited Warwick's pleasure, but with no result. Heralds were sent challenging the Earl to come forth with his army and settle the issue between himself and his former pupil, but to no avail. Finally, Edward in full armour went himself to the gate-towers and dared Richard Neville to come forth and resolve their quarrel man to man, but answer came there none.

Having established his moral superiority at least, and learning that his brother George of Clarence was approaching from the south at the head of 4,000 men, and that Montagu was now closing on Coventry, Edward led his army away south to meet his brother. Secret exchanges between the three sons of Cecily Neville had made clear to Edward that Clarence was no longer contented with his lot as Warwick's puppet and was minded to join with his brothers again. Their forces met at Banbury and here the two armies united and Edward, proclaiming his claim to the kingship, immediately marched on London where the City Fathers threw open the gates to him. They welcomed the return of the handsome, free-spending young King, who lost little time in visiting Westminster to see his wife and his first-born son, before ensuring that Henry VI was returned to his former chambers in the Tower. Then the returned King gave all his formidable energies to summoning every fighting man within short march of London to join with him in his rightful cause, for Edward knew that now Richard Neville and he must presently fight, and to the death.

Early on the morning of Saturday April 13th, Richard of Gloucester led the vanguard of the King's host out of London's Aldergate and marched up the well-trodden way towards St Albans. For the last time in England's history, an army of York tramped northwards out of London to meet their approaching Lancastrian enemies, and this time they would meet short of St Albans, at a village called Barnet, where they would fight to a finish - supremest bitter irony - on the Easter Day of 1471.

The day after Edward had moved away from Coventry towards Banbury and thence to London, John Neville joined his brother giving Warwick some 15,000 men in all with which to settle accounts with the King he had made and unmade. The great Earl did not consider waiting for any further reinforcement which might, or might not, come from Somerset gathering men in the southwest, or from Jasper Tudor still recruiting in Wales. His estimate was that the men he had were more than enough to overwhelm the King, who he and his brother knew well would not stand siege behind London's walls. Edward's way was ever to seek quick battle and in this, Richard Neville would, at last, give him satisfaction. With John de Vere leading, Warwick and Montagu in the centre, and Exeter with the rearguard, under the banners of Lancaster, Warwick and Neville, the army moved briskly south towards St Albans.

Reaching Dunstable - of fateful memory - on Good Friday, Warwick had news of Edward's triumphant entry into London, and pushed on with all haste, taking a south-easterly route to interpose between the King and any reinforcement from Norfolk, ever-faithful to the Yorkist cause. His path took him from the traditional Watling Street approach towards and across the Great North Road and south again, reaching Monken Hadley, with his advance scouts in the village of Barnet by the early evening of Saturday, April 13th. Here Warwick's cavalry clashed with a superior force riding under the banner of Gloucester and retired hurriedly to their main force, which had reached the ridge overlooking and crossing the main road to the capital. It is, reputedly, the highest point between York and London and here Warwick decided to stand and await Edward's onslaught.

John de Vere, Earl of Oxford, was eager to maintain their line of advance arguing that an attack on Edward's smaller force would, at worst, force him aside and permit the Lancastrians to move further southeast and link with the Bastard of Fauconberg's Kentish men already advancing to join Warwick's main body. The Duke of Exeter agreed with this thinking, he had bitter memories of years of penniless exile and the accounting with York was long overdue. And how could Warwick know that Edward would attack their strong defensive position ? Was it not more likely that he would retreat back to London and behind those mighty walls outwait Lancaster's forces as he had done 10 years earlier ?

Richard and John Neville exchanged glances, they knew Edward Plantagenet better than their new Lancastrian allies. When the morning light broke, the Yorkist King and his brother would come rushing and Oxford and Exeter would have as much fighting as they could handle - perhaps too much. Their army would maintain its position in three divisions across the brow of the ridge, lining a hedge which ran across from Hadley Wood on their left to the sharp slope on the right. Oxford would command the right wing, Exeter the left and John Neville, Marquess Montagu, with his Yorkshiremen would hold the centre. Richard Neville, Earl of Warwick and Salisbury, would take his customary place behind the main fighting line with the reserves. As at Towton, the army ate, rested and, where the men could, slept in the ranks and awaited the dawn of Easter Day and the coming of Edward the King.

Arms of the Kings of England,
the Leopards of England quartered with the Lilies of France,
borne by Henry VI, Edward IV and Richard III.

CHAPTER TWENTY-ONE

"And...right early, each came upon other; and there was such a great mist that neither of them might see other perfectly."
[Warkworth Chronicle]

The Yorkist army had reached Warwick's position just as night fell on the Saturday evening. Gloucester, leading, had swung right when he met the firm resistance of the men lining the hedge and quickly formed the wing of Edward's army facing the Duke of Exeter's division. The King himself led the mainward of his army and sent George of Clarence to guard King Henry who, as had become customary, was made to ride with his captors to lend legitimacy to their cause. Dependable William Hastings led the rearguard and positioned his division on Edward's left, as he had done long before at Mortimer's Cross, and the Yorkists settled for the night.

In the darkness, Edward made two errors in the placing of his troops : first, his line was too close to Warwick's for comfort and, not wishing to make - or attract - a night attack, the Yorkist men were ordered to remain silent despite any provocation and to light no fires. In the event, this accidental location proved to Edward's advantage, since when Warwick's artillerymen opened spasmodic fire through the night to disturb their opponents' rest, they assumed the Yorkist line to be much further back than it was and their shot fell safely behind the ranks of fighting-men.

The second fault with the King's placing of his army, however, was potentially disastrous. When Richard of Gloucester had located the enemy's front rank and swung right to bring the army into line directly facing the men of Lancaster, in the blackness of the night he had taken his division too far to the right and could not see that his wing overlapped the division directly opposing him by a considerable margin. This unwitting placement was not disadvantageous for Gloucester's men, but since the whole Yorkist army had followed the young Duke's lead, its left wing was similarly outflanked by Lancaster's right. And, commanding the opposing force on that side of the field was John de Vere, the 'shooting star' of Oxford, who, despite cautious Warwick's strictures, had no intention of standing on the defensive when there was light enough to see and fight by.

BARNET. April 14th 1471. First Phase.

As daylight came, on the anniversary of the Resurrection, it revealed nothing of the misplacing of the opposing armies. A thick ground mist swirled between and around the two lines who could hear but not see their enemies and in these circumstances, the main responsibility for directing the movements of the forces fell to the immediate commanders. King Edward's orders to Hastings and Gloucester had been to close with the enemy to their front as soon as it was daylight and, with fierce shouts and trumpeting, the three Yorkist divisions lurched forward into the mist, probing for their antagonists. John Neville, mindful of his brother's overall plan, held his men in their place at the centre of Lancaster's line and took the shock of Edward's first charge, holding their ground as the familiar hammering of steel on steel started and grew to its usual deafening pitch.

The Earl of Oxford, immediately on hearing the battle cries to his front, ordered his own line to charge and met the advancing foemen head on, except on their extreme right, where their attack met no resistance. The men could hear the growing fury of battle to their left and swung inwards, searching for the source of the clangour, a manoeuvre which brought their full weight down on Hastings' flank and rear. Finding themselves under attack from every direction, Lord Hastings' division crumbled and fled from the field, back towards Barnet village and on towards London, with Oxford's men in hot triumphant pursuit. For one third of the King's army, the fight was already over.

And now the mist which had played Edward cruelly false, became his saving grace. Neither he, nor Montagu opposite, realised that the Yorkist left wing had been broken and both sides simply continued their own vicious hand-to-hand fight in the centre, without regard for what was happening on either flank. Meantime, Richard of Gloucester, not yet 20 years old and fighting his first major battle had, like Oxford, plunged forward to the attack and found half his blow falling on empty space. Hearing the noise of battle to his left, he worked his line round in that direction and, though hampered at first by marshy and adversely sloping ground, succeeded in pushing Exeter's line back and back, forcing this flank to extend and to lengthen until it had drawn in all Warwick's reserve.

After two hours of bitter fighting, with Edward and Montagu continually dressing their centre divisions to maintain their line with Gloucester and Exeter, the battle had swung round through 90 degrees, and still neither side showed any sign of giving way. And then, the decisive moment, John de Vere

BARNET. April 14th 1471. Second Phase.

Wrotham Wood.

To Hatfield.

WARWICK KILLED HERE

To St Albans

Hadley Wood.

To Enfield.

GLOUCESTER

EXETER

EDWARD

MONTAGUE

OXFORD

London and Barnet

N

realised that the battle he had assumed to be won following the success of his own charge, was still continuing, hammer and tongs, and a mile and more behind him and his men. Desperately shouting to captains and knights, sergeants and squires, he managed to collect most of his division again, pushed and ordered and bullied them into some kind of formation and led them back, through the clearing swathes of mist, towards the warring battle lines.

His division crashed back into the fight at the nearest point of contact, which, unhappily for Lancaster, was now the flank and rear of John Neville's division. The Yorkshiremen saw among the attacking ranks the shooting star banners of de Vere and, in the still uncertain light, mistook them for the Sunne in Splendour device of King Edward. With light enough at last to shoot by, Montagu's bowmen showered arrows on Oxford's men, who, recognising their attackers as their newly-found - and mistrusted - allies from the Nevilles' country, raised the all-too-familiar cry in these Wars of "Treason. Treason."

Oxford's men, believing half their army had turned its coat, turned away from the battle and ran, but their attack had already wrought its mischief and Montagu's line, reeling under the new attack, frightened and confused by the shouts of "Treason", began to recoil from the continuing pressure of Edward's centre. Ever the supreme fighting-man, King Edward felt the weakening of the enemy line and hurled himself and his men into the fray with the increased vigour which comes from a sense of impending victory after a hard-fought contest. Richard of Gloucester's division likewise found the antagonists to their front weakening, falling back, breaking, running.

Henry Holland, striving still to rally his wing, fell desperately wounded and was borne away by his close servants. John de Vere, whose fortune had swung from the height of victory to the depth of defeat in a single morning, was carried along in the surging retreat of his men and lived to fight another day. His hour would come in a later decade on a wooded hill in Leicestershire, when his victory would end forever the rule of the House of Plantagenet. Meantime, John Neville, trapped in the centre of a collapsing battle-line, his army dissolving around him, knew his time was all but spent and turned at bay. Not for him the plea for mercy of an all-conquering King, and he stood and fought and died.

When the scavengers stripped his corpse, they found his old Neville surcoat under the ripped and bloody Montagu mantle he had worn to lead his last battle. Some said it was to aid his escape should the day go against him, others knew he had died as he had lived, true to his Middleham blood-line.

Richard Neville, seeing the day was lost, his personal guard fleeing before the angry, advancing spears of the King, turned away and made for the horse lines in the woods to the rear. He cursed the persuasion of his brother who had said it would encourage the men to see their leaders ready to fight afoot alongside them, as he struggled to make good his escape, and in heavy plate-armour his effort was to no avail. He was caught by swift-running archers in their light leather jacks and carrying the long, steel knives they knew so well how to use and he went down under their concerted rush, just as he reached the illusory safety of the trees fringing the woods.

The life of Richard Neville, Earl of Warwick and Salisbury, richest and most powerful noble in the land, King's Lieutenant, Ruler of England, maker and unmaker of Kings, ended at the hands of unknown, common soldiers, whose only esteem for their victim was for the richness of his armour and weapons.

Recovered after the battle on specific orders of the King, the bodies of the two Nevilles were carried back to London and displayed, naked, in open coffins on the steps of St Paul's cathedral, so that the world might see there was now but one Ruler in England, and his name was Edward the King.

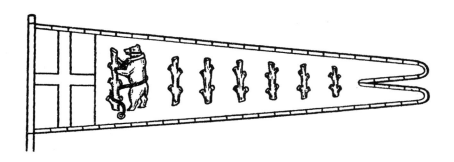

Standard of Richard Neville, Earl of Warwick

CHAPTER TWENTY-TWO

... and Endings.

Although Richard Neville had gone to meet his own maker, his legacy to those he had left behind was a troubled inheritance. George of Clarence, his son-in-law, had seized all Warwick's estates in the aftermath of Barnet and for more than a year disputed ownership with his younger brother, Richard of Gloucester, who, over Clarence's vehement protests and obstruction had insisted on marrying Anne Neville, widowed at Tewkesbury, three weeks after Barnet, and co-heiress to Warwick's lands. In the end, following the King's intevention on several occasions, Clarence grudgingly agreed that Richard should have Middleham and the northern estates, including Barnard Castle, while he kept the rich, broad acres in the Midlands and into Wales, and, oddly, Richmond Castle as a last toehold in the north.

The claims of the young Duke of Bedford, George Neville, son of Montagu and erstwhile affianced husband of the King's eldest child, Elizabeth, as son of a traitor, were easily put aside. He was eventually stripped of his semi-royal title on grounds that he had not the wealth to sustain it, and Richard of Gloucester took the penniless young man into his own household. There he died in 1484, with few, if any, to remember that, briefly, he had been heir to the throne of England.

The Archbishop of York, the older George Neville, made his peace with King Edward after Barnet, but was caught out a year later plotting against the crown with George of Clarence, another who never really recovered from being briefly touched by glory when named heir to England's throne. Unwilling to involve his brother in a public trial, Edward contented himself with confiscation of the Archbishop's wealth - a vast amount of money and treasure - and exiled him to the fortress of Hammes in the pale of Calais. Three years later, he was released on the personal plea of Richard of Gloucester, but his health never recovered and he died in the June of 1476 at Blyth in Northumberland.

Anne Beauchamp, widow of the Kingmaker, Countess of Warwick in her own right, found all her vast properties were allocated to her two daughters and their husbands by a Parliamentary Bill which stipulated that her property should be partitioned "in like manner and form as if the Countess (of Warwick) were dead". She remained a virtual royal prisoner in the sanctuary of Beaulieu Abbey, until Richard prevailed on his brother to grant her a measure of freedom and allow her to end her days in the comparative comfort of Middleham and its estates. She survived her benefactor and her daughters, dying in 1490.

Anne and Isabel took after their mother's side, the tender bloom of the Beauchamps being always more apparent in them than the Neville hardiness of their father. Isabel gave Clarence two heirs who survived childhood, Edward and Margaret, before she died at Christmastide, 1476, still short of her thirtieth year. She was spared the disgrace and death of her husband, little over a year later in February 1478. Edward had finally tired of his brother's constant plotting and scheming and, pressed by his wife and her family to put an end to the matter, had accused, judged and condemned George of Clarence of high treason and the "false, fleeting, perjur'd" Duke was put down within the Tower's walls the same day.

Their children met equally unhappy fates. The boy, Edward, was created Earl of Warwick by the King following the execution of his father, but the Clarence title was allowed to lapse. Following Henry Tudor's unlikely triumph at Bosworth, the young Earl was incarcerated in the Tower until, years later, the Spanish envoys negotiating the Infanta, Catherine of Aragon's betrothal to Arthur, Henry's oldest son, intimated concern at the continuing existence of one nearer to the throne than the projected husband. Henry VII, never a man to let quibbles stand in the way of his will, trumped up a conspiracy charge and Warwick was beheaded.

His sister, Margaret, lived longer and in due time became a favourite with the second Tudor King, Henry VIII, who created her Countess of Salisbury and declared her to be the saintliest woman in England. However, like many others before and after her, she found that the intimate friendship of the Tudors was a dangerous distinction in the long term and 'Bluff Hal' sent her, and her eldest son, Lord Montagu, to the block when she was old and sick and helpless, lest she should provide a focal point for unrest against the King's majesty.

Anne Neville lived to see her husband crowned King of England and their only child, another Edward, created Prince of Wales. Less happily, in the early Spring of 1484, while she and King Richard were residing at Nottingham Castle, they learned their son had died suddenly at Middleham and Queen Anne never recovered from the bitterness of the blow. She died in the March of the following year and thus, like her sister, did not live to see her husband's tragic end, his crown toppled by traitors and his corpse dishonoured by lesser men.

Cecily Neville, 'Proud Cis', the Rose of Raby, outlived all her sons and lived to see her granddaughter Elizabeth married to Henry Tudor and made Queen of England as she herself might once have been. She died in 1495, a lonely old lady, having latterly lived a life of monastic piety and self-denial, at her Berkhamstead Castle. Warwick's sister Eleanor, wife to Thomas, Lord Stanley, the master-trimmer, died before her husband, but not before giving him children who, in the course of time, continued and stablished the line of Earls of Derby. And the youngest sister of Richard Neville, Margaret, married John de Vere, so becoming Countess of Oxford and wife to the one great general to fight on the side of Lancaster.

Thus the descendants of Earl Ralph, most uxorious of all the Nevilles, continued to multiply and thrive, albeit, perhaps, in less spectacular fashion than had their forebears. And some of them continue so to do to the present day. But the first ones, the Nevilles cursed by the pride of Beaufort blood-royal in their veins - the Lordly Ones who dwelled for a time in the great Hollow Hills of Middleham and Barnard, Carlisle and Dunstanburgh, Sheriff Hutton and Warwick - endured for a space, and were gone.

"The Beginning ..." Penrith Castle

(Geoffrey Wheeler)

ACKNOWLEDGEMENTS

I said before, in The Hollow Crowns, that acknowledgements of help and support had been authoritatively described as an over-effusion of false modesty on the part of the writer. I did not believe it then, and still less now. One should *always* say please and thank you.

So, sincere gratitude to Christine Symonds and Carolyn Hammond for their ever-willing support and advice on source material. Much of the base material for this book comes from my own resources, written and mental [thank the good Lord, my memory for events which took place more than 500 years ago seems vastly superior to my recollection of what happened yesterday] but I owe a great debt to these ladies, the guardians of the Richard III Society's libraries, for their help.

Special thanks again to Geoffrey Wheeler for his willingness to share his enormous archive of illustrative material and to give his uniquely expert advice on sources and all other matters connected with the appropriate "decoration" of a book. I asked for his help with The Lordly Ones at what was a very fraught time for him, since he was, simultaneously, organising a major exhibit for the Richard III Society, but his response to me could not have been speedier or more helpful.

In this particular context, I must also thank, most sincerely, the Society of Antiquaries of London for their kind permission to include the "twin" portraits of Edward IV and Richard III in the book.

In my efforts to ensure accuracy of content and presentation, I have been fortunate in securing the help of two experts in the field of medieval authorship: Pam Benstead of Kempsey, Worcester, and Susan Ingham of Blackburn, who very kindly read through the book's second proof and made invaluable suggestions and corrections. Dear ladies, my thanks to you both in brimming measure.

And last – but far from least – my thanks to the Ladies of Middleham Castle. In particular, to Sue Constantine, who suggested retirement would be a waste when such an interesting subject awaited exploration, and to Maureen Bush whose encouragement throughout the writing period has been a continual source of strength.

SOURCES

These could be described in the usual classic terms: "many and varied", "too numerous to mention" and so on. However, apart from my own abundant jottings – often (unhappily) not attributed at the time of writing – I am mainly indebted [in no particular order of importance or preference] to the following:

Anciently: The Warkworth Chronicle. Polydore Vergil,
      the Crowland Continuations, the Paston Letters,
      the Arrivall of King Edward IV,
      Bentley's Excerpta Historica;

Less
Anciently: Warwick, by Charles Oman,
      Various Papers by Lockwood Huntley
      English History (Blacks Historical Sources)

More
Modernly: Warwick the Kingmaker by Paul Kendall,
      Battlefields (and More Battlefields) of England
      by Alfred H. Burne,
      North-Eastern England During the Wars of
      the Roses by A. J. Pollard.

Index

Also available from Baildon Books

Geoffrey Richardson's

THE HOLLOW CROWNS

For the first time – all major battles of the Wars of the Roses
in detail and in one volume.

From the fields and gardens by St Albans on an early Summer's day in 1455, to the death of the last Plantagenet King of England, alone, betrayed and hopelessly mired in marshland below Bosworth's Ambion Hill, the reader is swept along through three decades of English History.

Encountering along the way: the hapless Henry VI, pathetic son of the victor of Agincourt; Margaret of Anjou, Henry's Queen and Lancaster's champion for 20 years; Richard Neville, fabled Kingmaker Warwick, who – the story shows – has enjoyed a greater reputation in history than his deeds warranted; the giant Edward IV, England's greatest Warrior-King, and Richard, his youngest brother, arguably the last true monarch of England and almost certainly the worst-slandered.

This all-new account of the bloodiest 30 years in English History has been termed: "History made easy – and interesting!" Written in a fresh narrative style, with full-page, "3D" Battlemaps of all eleven major conflicts and portraits of the principal participants (including line-drawings of Warwick and Margaret of Anjou developed from computer-enhanced sources) "THE HOLLOW CROWNS" puts the story back into History.

ISBN 0 9527621 0 2

£5.99

AND ...

Geoffrey Richardson's

"THE DECEIVERS"

This History covers the last two years of the internecine struggle between York and Lancaster – the so-called Wars of the Roses – from the death of Edward IV in April 1483, to the defeat and death of his successor, Richard III, at Bosworth, and through the early years of the usurper, Henry Tudor, to the end of the 15th Century.

Written in this author's easy narrative style,
"The Deceivers" sets out to answer four main questions:

- *Why was the life of William, Lord Hastings ended so abruptly and ingloriously by his former comrade-in-arms –*

- *Why should Henry Stafford, second Duke of Buckingham, rebel against the King he had helped to his throne three months earlier -*

- *How could a seasoned warrior like Richard III lose the Battle of Bosworth against what was, at best, a "rabble in arms" –*

and, most important of all,

- *Who killed the Princes in the Tower, and When, and Why –*

The answers to all these questions are set down in "The Deceivers" and reveal a stunning conspiracy on the part of a handful of people, who have never previously been indicted for the crimes of which they are guilty, but who changed the course of English History.

ISBN 09527621 1 0

£5.99

135

What the media had to say about ...

"THE HOLLOW CROWNS"

"... it is in *The Hollow Crowns'* vivid descriptions of the wars' 11 major battles that Richardson shows his considerable ability as a researcher and writer. He provides easily understandable explanations of the courses of the battles themselves, displaying an expert knowledge of such decisive factors as topography, weather conditions and weaponry. In addition Richardson presents in an entertaining and comprehensible manner, the complex and highly fluid relationships between the numerous characters involved ... As an alternative view of a well-known and turbulent time, *The Hollow Crowns* is highly recommended to anyone interested in medieval warfare, the history of England, or the foibles of royalty." (MILITARY HISTORY MAGAZINE)

"... No-one really understands the battles of the Wars of the Roses. There were too many of them and it is hard to remember who is on whose side, especially when some participants change horses in mid-stream. Thanks to Geoffrey Richardson's book, all is explained ... the descriptions bring the battles to immediate life making it easy to visualise what it must have been like ... What comes through is the author's love of his subject and his immense knowledge ..." (AFFINITY, Sydney Australia)

"The book is above all a good read ... the information is provided in a simple format with good battle maps and illustrations to aid the reader in appreciating the ground over which the Wars of the Roses battles were fought. For the medieval military enthusiast one could find no better book than this with which to start deeper research into the subject. It is written in a lively style by a man who is very keen on his subject and this shines through in the narrative style of his writing which he uses to good effect ..." (Andrew Boardman, author of "The Battle of Towton" etc etc, BATTLEFIELD PRESS)

"THE DECEIVERS"

"... The author, who has been fascinated by history since he was a schoolboy has treated the book as an enthralling detective story ... making the subject interesting and entertaining ... He makes a persuasive case for Richard III and pins the blame [for the Princes' murder] on the plotting of three 15th century schemers ...[He says] I am writing about events that happened 500 years ago, but people were driven then by the same things that drive them now - ambition, pride and desire for power ..." (EVENING COURIER)